ARCHITECTURE AND BUILDING

Ferguson
An imprint of Infobase Publishing

Ferguson
An imprint of Infobase Publishing
132 West 31st Street
New York NY 10001

ISBN-10: 0-8160-6569-1
ISBN-13: 978-0-8160-6569-1

Library of Congress Cataloging-in-Publication Data

Careers in focus. Architecture and building.
    p. cm.
  Includes index.
  ISBN 978-0-8160-6569-1 (hc)
   1. Architecture—Vocational guidance—United States. 2. Building trades—
Vocational guidance—United States. I. J. G. Ferguson Publishing Company. II.
Title: Architecture and building.
  NA1995.C28 2007
  720.23'73—dc22   2006033421

Ferguson books are available at special discounts when purchased in bulk quantities for businesses, associations, institutions, or sales promotions. Please call our Special Sales Department in New York at (212) 967-8800 or (800) 322-8755.

You can find Ferguson on the World Wide Web at http://www.fergpubco.com

Text design by David Strelecky
Cover design by Takeshi Takahashi

Printed in the United States of America

MP MSRF 10 9 8 7 6 5 4 3 2 1

This book is printed on acid-free paper.

Table of Contents

Introduction 1

Architects 5

Carpenters 14

Civil Engineers 23

College Professors, Architecture 31

Computer-Aided Design Drafters
and Technicians 40

Construction Inspectors 49

Construction Managers 56

Cost Estimators 63

Drafters 70

Electricians 78

Environmental Engineers 86

Heating and Cooling Technicians 94

Historic Preservationists 108

Interior Designers and Decorators 120

Landscape Architects 131

Office Clerks 140

Plumbers and Pipefitters 146

Surveyors 152

Urban and Regional Planners 160

Writers, Architecture & Construction 171

Index 183

Introduction

Almost anywhere you look—be it a skyscraper, department store, museum, school, factory, church, hospital, or just a cozy bungalow on your block—you can see the work of architects and builders. Highly trained professionals imagined, designed, and built every structure we use in our everyday lives. And architects and builders don't just focus on buildings but also bridges, highways, and other transportation systems, as well as countless other structures and systems we sometimes take for granted.

Opportunities are available for those interested in pursuing design and engineering careers (architects, civil engineers, environmental engineers, interior designers, and landscape designers), those interested in working in building careers (carpenters, construction managers, cost estimators, electricians, heating and cooling technicians, plumbers, and surveyors), those interested in preserving endangered places (historic preservationists), and those interested in developing and redeveloping cities, metropolitan areas, or entire regions (planners). There are also opportunities in education and journalism.

Earnings in architecture and building range from less than $15,000 for beginning office clerks to more than $120,000 for top architects and civil engineers.

Careers in architecture and building are available to those with a wide variety of educational backgrounds. For example, you will only need a high school diploma to work as an office clerk. Many building-related careers, such as carpenters, electricians, heating and cooling technicians, and plumbers, require the completion of a formal apprenticeship. Other architecture and building careers require some postsecondary training (computer-aided design drafter, cost estimator, and surveyor), an associate's degree (interior designer) or a bachelor's degree (architect, civil engineer, environmental engineer, landscape architect, and planner). College professors must have at least a master's degree to teach at four-year institutions.

The construction industry is one of the largest in the United States. According to the U.S. Department of Labor, it employed 7 million wage and salary workers in 2004. The department predicts that employment in the construction industry will grow by 11 percent through 2014—slightly slower than the average for all industries through 2014. Despite this prediction, there will continue to be a steady expansion of the market for construction services. Although further technological improvements in construction methods and equipment are expected to raise the productivity of workers, the volume of activity will require substantial numbers of craftworkers in the various building trades, mostly as replacements for those who retire or leave the labor force for other reasons. The U.S. Department of Labor predicts that employment will be especially strong for the following workers in architecture and building: construction inspectors, cost estimators, environmental engineers, and heating and cooling technicians. The department predicts that employment for architects will grow about as fast as the average, while employment for landscape architects is expected to grow faster than the average.

Although prospects look promising, the construction industry is very sensitive to fluctuations in the national economy. These fluctuations usually affect part-time and seasonal workers and lower-skilled workers the most. Skilled, artistic tradespeople, however, are almost always in demand, even during economic downturns.

Each article in *Careers in Focus: Architecture & Building* discusses a particular architecture and building career in detail. The articles appear in Ferguson's *Encyclopedia of Careers and Vocational Guidance* but have been updated and revised with the latest information from the U.S. Department of Labor, professional organizations, and other sources. The articles College Professors, Architecture; Construction Managers; Historic Preservationists; and Writers, Architecture & Construction were written specifically for this book. The following paragraphs detail the sections and features that appear in the book.

The **Quick Facts** section provides a brief summary of each career, including recommended school subjects, personal skills, work environments, minimum educational requirements, salary ranges, certification or licensing requirements, and employment outlook. This section also provides acronyms and identification numbers for the following government classification indexes: the Dictionary of Occupational Titles (DOT), the Guide to Occupational Exploration (GOE), the National Occupational Classification (NOC) Index, and the Occupational Information Network (O*NET)-Standard Occupational Classification System (SOC) index. The DOT, GOE, and O*NET-SOC indexes have been created by the U.S. government; the NOC index is Canada's career classification system. Readers can use the identification numbers listed in the Quick Facts section to access further information about a career. Print editions of the DOT (*Dictionary of Occupational Titles*. Indianapolis, Ind.: JIST Works, 1991) and GOE (*The Complete Guide for Occupational*

Exploration. Indianapolis, Ind.: JIST Works, 1993) are available at libraries. Electronic versions of the NOC (http://www23.hrdc-drhc. gc.ca) and O*NET-SOC (http://online.onetcenter.org) are available on the Internet. When no DOT, GOE, NOC, or O*NET-SOC numbers are present, this means that the U.S. Department of Labor or Human Resources Development Canada have not created a numerical designation for this career. In this instance, you will see the acronym "N/A" or not available.

The **Overview** section is a brief introductory description of the duties and responsibilities involved in this career. Oftentimes, a career may have a variety of job titles. When this is the case, alternative career titles are presented. The **History** section describes the history of the particular job as it relates to the overall development of its industry or field. **The Job** describes the primary and secondary duties of the job. **Requirements** discusses high school and postsecondary education and training requirements, any necessary certification or licensing, and other personal requirements for success in the job. **Exploring** offers suggestions on how to gain experience in or knowledge of the particular job before making a firm educational and financial commitment. The focus is on what can be done while still in high school (or in the early years of college) to gain a better understanding of the job. The **Employers** section gives an overview of typical places of employment for the job. **Starting Out** discusses the best ways to land that first job, be it through the college placement office, newspaper ads, or personal contact. The **Advancement** section describes what kind of career path to expect from the job and how to get there. **Earnings** lists salary ranges and describes the typical fringe benefits. The **Work Environment** section describes the typical surroundings and conditions of employment—whether indoors or outdoors, noisy or quiet, social or independent. Also discussed are typical hours worked, any seasonal fluctuations, and the stresses and strains of the job. The **Outlook** section summarizes the job in terms of the general economy and industry projections. For the most part, outlook information is obtained from the U.S. Bureau of Labor Statistics and is supplemented by information taken from professional associations. Job-growth terms follow those used in the *Occupational Outlook Handbook*. Growth described as "much faster than the average" means an increase of 27 percent or more. Growth described as "faster than the average" means an increase of 18 to 26 percent. Growth described as "about as fast as the average" means an increase of 9 to 17 percent. Growth described as "more slowly than the average" means an increase of 0 to 8 percent. "Decline" means a decrease by any amount. Each article ends with **For More Information,** which lists organizations that provide information on training, education, internships, scholarships, and job placement.

Careers in Focus: Architecture & Building also includes photos, informative sidebars, and interviews with professionals in the field.

Architects

OVERVIEW

Architects plan, design, and observe construction of facilities used for human occupancy and of other structures. They consult with clients, plan layouts of buildings, prepare drawings of proposed buildings, write specifications, and prepare scale and full-sized drawings. Architects also may help clients obtain bids, select contractors, and negotiate construction contracts, and they also visit construction sites to ensure that the work is being completed according to specification. There are approximately 129,000 architects working in the United States.

HISTORY

Architecture began not with shelters for people to live in but with the building of religious structures—from Stonehenge in England and the pyramids in Egypt to pagodas in Japan and the Parthenon in Greece. It was the Romans who developed a new building method—concrete vaulting—that made possible large cities with permanent masonry buildings. As they extended the Roman Empire, they built for public and military purposes. They developed and built apartment buildings, law courts, public baths, theaters, and circuses. The Industrial Revolution, with its demand for factories and mills, developed iron and steel construction, which evolved into the steel and glass skyscraper of today.

Because the history of architecture follows that of human civilization, the architecture of any period reflects the culture of its people. Architecture of early periods has influenced that of later centuries, including the work of contemporary architects. The field continues to develop as new techniques and materials are discovered and as architects blend creativity with function.

THE JOB

The architect normally has two responsibilities: to design a building that will satisfy the client and to protect the public's health, safety, and welfare. The second responsibility requires architects to be licensed by the states in which they work. Meeting the first responsibility involves many steps. The job begins with learning what the client wants. The architect takes many factors into consideration, including local and state building and design regulations, climate, soil on which the building is to be constructed, zoning laws, fire regulations, and the client's financial limitations.

The architect then prepares a set of plans that, upon the client's approval, will be developed into final design and construction documents. The final design shows the exact dimensions of every portion of the building, including the location and size of columns and beams, electrical outlets and fixtures, plumbing, heating and air-conditioning facilities, windows, and doors. The architect works closely with consulting engineers on the specifics of the plumbing, heating, air conditioning, and electrical work to be done.

The architect then assists the client in getting bids from general contractors, one of whom will be selected to construct the building to the specifications. The architect helps the client through the completion of the construction and occupancy phases, making certain that the correct materials are used and that the drawings and specifications are faithfully followed.

Throughout the process, the architect works closely with a design or project team. This team is usually made up of the following: *designers,* who specialize in design development; a *structural designer,* who designs the frame of the building in accordance with the work of the architect; the *project manager* or *job superintendent,* who sees that the full-detail drawings are completed to the satisfaction of the architect; and the *specification writer* and *estimator,* who prepare a project manual that describes in more detail the materials to be used in the building, their quality and method of installation, and all details related to the construction of the building.

The architect's job is very complex. He or she is expected to know construction methods, engineering principles and practices, and materials. Architects also must be up to date on new design and construction techniques and procedures. Although architects once spent most of their time designing buildings for the wealthy, they are now more often involved in the design of housing developments, individual dwellings, supermarkets, industrial plants, office

Other Career Options for Architecture Students

Students with educational backgrounds in architecture not only become architects but also can enter the following related careers:

Animator
Architectural Critic
Architectural
    Photographer
Architectural Programmer
Architectural Renderer
Building Inspector
Building Pathologist
CAD Coordinator
Campus Planner
Cartographer
City Planner
Civil Engineer
Construction Inspector
Construction Manager

Contractor
Corporate Consultant
Developer
Environmental Planner
Industrial Designer
Lawyer
Model Maker
Museum Curator
Property Assessor
Real Estate Agent
Real Estate Project
    Manager
Set Designer
Structural Engineer
Technical Writer

Source: American Institute of Architecture Students

buildings, shopping centers, air terminals, schools, banks, museums, churches, and dozens of other types of buildings.

Architects may specialize in any one of a number of fields, including building appraisal, city planning, teaching, architectural journalism, furniture design, lighting design, or government service. Regardless of the area of specialization, the architect's major task is understanding the client's needs and then reconciling them into a meaningful whole.

REQUIREMENTS

High School

To prepare for this career while in high school, take a college preparatory program that includes courses in English, mathematics, physics, art (especially freehand drawing), social studies, history, and foreign languages. Courses in business and computer science also will be useful.

Postsecondary Training

Because most state architecture registration boards require a professional degree, high school students are advised early in their senior year to apply for admission to a professional program accredited by the National Architectural Accrediting Board. Competition to enter these programs is high. Grades, class rank, and aptitude and achievement scores count heavily in determining who will be accepted.

Most schools of architecture offer degrees through either a five-year bachelor's program, a three- or four-year master's program, or a two-year master of architecture program for students who have earned a preprofessional undergraduate degree in architecture or a related area. The majority of architecture students seek out the bachelor's degree in architecture, going from high school directly into a five-year program. Though this is the fastest route, you should be certain that you want to study architecture. Because the programs are so specialized, it is difficult to transfer to another field of study if you change your mind. The master's degree option allows for more flexibility but takes longer to complete. In this case, students first earn a liberal arts degree and then continue their training by completing a master's program in architecture.

A typical college architecture program includes courses in architectural history and theory, the technical and legal aspects of building design, science, and liberal arts.

Certification or Licensing

All states and the District of Columbia require that individuals be licensed before contracting to provide architectural services in that particular state. Though many work in the field without licensure, only licensed architects are required to take legal responsibility for all work. Using a licensed architect for a project is, therefore, less risky than using an unlicensed one. Architects who are licensed usually take on projects with larger responsibilities and have greater chances to advance to managerial or executive positions.

The requirements for registration include graduation from an accredited school of architecture and three years of practical experience (called an internship) with a licensed architect. (All states, except Arizona, use the training standards of the Intern Development Program, a branch of the American Institute of Architects and the National Council of Architectural Registration Boards.) After these requirements are met, individuals can take the rigorous four-day Architect Registration Examination. Some states require architects to maintain their licensing through continued education.

These individuals may complete a certain number of credits every year or two through seminars, workshops, university classes, self-study courses, or other sources.

In addition to becoming licensed, a growing number of architects choose to obtain certification by the National Council of Architectural Registration Boards (NCARB). If an architect plans to work in more than one state, obtaining this certification can make it easier to become licensed in different states. Approximately one-third of all licensed architects have earned the NCARB certification.

Other Requirements

If you are interested in architecture, you should be intelligent, observant, responsible, and self-disciplined. You should have a concern for detail and accuracy, the ability to communicate effectively both orally and in writing, and the ability to accept criticism constructively. Although great artistic ability is not necessary, you should be able to visualize spatial relationships and have the capacity to solve technical problems. Mathematical ability is also important. In addition, you should possess organizational skills and leadership qualities and be able to work well with others.

EXPLORING

Most architects welcome the opportunity to talk with young people interested in entering architecture. You may be able to visit their offices to can gain firsthand knowledge of the type of work done by architects. You can also visit a design studio of a school of architecture or work for an architect or building contractor during summer vacations. Also, many architecture schools offer summer programs for high school students. Books and magazines on architecture also can give you a broad understanding of the nature of the work and the values of the profession.

EMPLOYERS

Of the 129,000 architects working in the United States, most are employed by architectural firms or other firms related to the construction industry. About one in four architects, however, are self-employed—the ultimate dream of many people in the profession. A few develop graphic design, interior design, or product specialties. Still others put their training to work in the theater, film, or television fields or in museums, display firms, and architectural product and materials manufacturing companies. A small number

Famous Architects on the Web

Daniel Burnham
http://www.ci.chi.il.us/Landmarks/Architects/Burnham.html
http://www.architechgallery.com/arch_info/artists_pages/
    daniel_burnham_bio.html

Paulo Mendes da Rocha
http://www.pritzkerprize.com/2006/pdf/photobook.pdf

Frank Gehry
http://www.pritzkerprize.com/gehry.htm

Walter Burley Griffin
http://www.ci.chi.il.us/Landmarks/Architects/Griffin.html

Zaha Hadid
http://www.pritzkerprize.com

Jens Jensen
http://www.jensjensen.org

Philip Johnson
http://www.pritzkerprize.com

Julia Morgan
http://architecture.about.com/library/bl-morgan.htm

Frederick Law Olmsted
http://fredericklawolmsted.com

I.M. Pei
http://www.pritzkerprize.com/pei.htm

Mies van der Rohe
http://www.ci.chi.il.us/Landmarks/Architects/VanDerRohe.html
http://www.moma.org/exhibitions/2001/mies

Louis Sullivan
http://www.ci.chi.il.us/Landmarks/Architects/Sullivan.html
http://web.mit.edu/museum/chicago/sullivan.html

Jorn Utzon
http://www.pritzkerprize.com

Paul Williams
http://architecture.about.com/library/bl-williams.htm

Frank Lloyd Wright
http://www.franklloydwright.org
http://www.wrightplus.org
http://www.ci.chi.il.us/Landmarks/Architects/Wright.html
http://www.architechgallery.com/arch_info/artists_pages/frank_
    lloyd_wright.html

are employed in government agencies such as the Departments of Defense, Interior, and Housing and Urban Development, and the General Services Administration.

STARTING OUT

Students entering architecture following graduation start as interns in an architectural office. As interns, they assist in preparing architectural construction documents. They also handle related details, such as administering contracts, coordinating the work of other professionals on the project, researching building codes and construction materials, and writing specifications. As an alternative to working for an architectural firm, some architecture graduates go into allied fields such as construction, engineering, interior design, landscape architecture, or real estate development.

ADVANCEMENT

Interns and architects alike are given progressively more complex jobs. Architects may advance to supervisory or managerial positions. Some architects become partners in established firms, while others take steps to establish their own practice.

EARNINGS

Architects earned a median annual salary of $62,850 in 2005, according to the U.S. Department of Labor. The lowest-paid 10 percent earned less than $39,130 annually, while the highest paid 10 percent earned $105,500 or more.

The American Institute of Architects (AIA) reports that the starting annual salary for graduates of schools of architecture working during their internship before licensing was approximately $30,000 in 2002.

Well-established architects who are partners in an architectural firm or who have their own businesses generally earn much more than salaried employees. According to the AIA, partners in very large firms can earn $132,000 or more a year. Most employers offer such fringe benefits as health insurance, sick and vacation pay, and retirement plans.

WORK ENVIRONMENT

Architects normally work a 40-hour week. There may be a number of times when they will have to work overtime, especially when under pressure to complete an assignment. Self-employed architects

Architects meet to discuss their latest project. *(Jon Riley/Index Stock Imagery)*

work fewer regular hours and often meet with clients in their homes or offices during the evening. Architects usually work in comfortable offices, but they may spend a considerable amount of time outside the office, visiting clients or viewing the progress of a particular job in the field. Their routines usually vary considerably.

OUTLOOK

Employment in the field is expected to grow about as fast as the average through 2014, according to the U.S. Department of Labor. The number of architects in demand will depend on the volume of construction. The construction industry is extremely sensitive to fluctuations in the overall economy, and a prolonged poor economic climate could result in layoffs. On the positive side, employment of architects is not likely to be affected by the growing use of computer technologies. Rather than replacing architects, computers are being used to enhance architects' work.

Competition for employment will continue to be strong, particularly in prestigious architectural firms. Openings will not be newly created positions but will become available as the workload increases and established architects transfer to other occupations or leave the field.

FOR MORE INFORMATION

For information on education, scholarships, and student membership opportunities, contact the following organizations:

American Institute of Architects
1735 New York Avenue, NW
Washington, DC 20006-5292
Tel: 800-AIA-3837
Email: infocentral@aia.org
http://www.aia.org

American Institute of Architecture Students
1735 New York Avenue, NW
Washington, DC 20006-5292
Tel: 202-626-7472
Email: mailbox@aias.org
http://www.aiasnatl.org

Association of Collegiate Schools of Architecture
1735 New York Avenue, NW
Washington, DC 20006-5292
Tel: 202-785-2324
Email: vlove@acsa-arch.org
http://www.acsa-arch.org

For information on certification, contact

National Council of Architectural Registration Boards
1801 K Street, NW, Suite 1100-K
Washington, DC 20006-1301
Tel: 202-783-6500
Email: customerservice@ncarb.org
http://www.ncarb.org

For information on careers in architecture, visit the following Web site:

Architecture Careers
http://www.archcareers.org

Carpenters

QUICK FACTS

School Subjects
Mathematics
Technical/shop

Personal Skills
Following instructions
Mechanical/manipulative

Work Environment
Indoors and outdoors
Primarily multiple locations

Minimum Education Level
Apprenticeship

Salary Range
$21,940 to $35,580 to
$60,910+

Certification or Licensing
Voluntary

Outlook
About as fast as the average

DOT
860

GOE
05.05.02

NOC
7271

O*NET-SOC
47-2031.00

OVERVIEW

Carpenters cut, shape, level, and fasten together pieces of wood and other construction materials, such as wallboard, plywood, and insulation. Many carpenters work on constructing, remodeling, or repairing houses and other kinds of buildings. Other carpenters work at construction sites where roads, bridges, docks, boats, mining tunnels, and wooden vats are built. They may specialize in building the rough framing of a structure, and thus be considered *rough carpenters,* or they may specialize in the finishing details of a structure, such as the trim around doors and windows, and be *finish carpenters.* Approximately 1.3 million carpenters work in the United States.

HISTORY

Wood has been used as a building material since the dawn of civilization. Tools that resembled modern hand tools first began to be made around 1500 B.C. By the Middle Ages, many of the basic techniques and the essential tools of carpentry were perfected, largely by monks in the early monasteries.

Over time, as local societies advanced, many specialties developed in the field of carpentry. The primary work came from building construction. Buildings were mostly built with braced-frame construction, which made use of large, heavy timbers held together with mortised joints and diagonal bracing. In this kind of construction, carpenters were often the principal workers on a house or other building.

Carpenters also were responsible for many of the necessities that kept their towns running day to day. Pit sawyers milled lumber from trees. Carts and wagons called for wheelwrights, who fabricated wheels and axles, and then, as transportation became more sophisticated, coachmakers and wagonmakers appeared. The increased use of brass and iron led to work for patternmakers, who created the wooden forms that were the first step in casting. On the domestic front, cabinetmakers and joiners were skilled in building furniture or creating interior trimwork.

It's no surprise that the role of carpenters has continued to change, largely due to the rise of machine technology. Since the mid-19th century, balloon-frame construction, which makes use of smaller and lighter pieces of wood, has simplified the construction process, and concrete and steel have replaced wood for many purposes, especially in floors and roofs. Power tools have replaced hand tools in many instances. But as some carpentry tasks in building construction have become easier, other new jobs, such as making forms for poured concrete, have added to the importance of carpenters at construction sites. Carpentry continues to be an important and necessary trade.

THE JOB

Carpenters remain the largest group of workers in the building trades—there are approximately 1.3 million carpenters in the United States today. The vast majority of them work for contractors involved in building, repairing, and remodeling buildings and other structures. Manufacturing firms, schools, stores, and government bodies employ most other carpenters.

Essentially, carpenters do two kinds of work: rough carpentry and finish carpentry. Rough carpenters construct and install temporary structures and supports and wooden structures used in industrial settings, as well as parts of buildings that are usually covered up when the rooms are finished. Among the structures built by such carpenters are scaffolds for other workers to stand on, chutes used as channels for wet concrete, forms for concrete foundations, and timber structures that support machinery. In buildings, they may put up the frame and install rafters, joists, subflooring, wall sheathing, prefabricated wall panels and windows, and many other components.

Finish carpenters install hardwood flooring, staircases, shelves, cabinets, trim on windows and doors, and other woodwork and hardware that make the building look complete, inside and outside. Finish carpentry requires especially careful, precise workmanship, since the result must have a good appearance in addition to being sturdy. Many carpenters employed by building contractors do both rough and finish work on buildings.

Although they do many different tasks in different settings, carpenters generally follow the same fundamental steps. First, they review blueprints or plans (or they obtain instructions from a supervisor) to determine the dimensions of the structure to be built and the types of materials to be used. Sometimes local building codes mandate how a structure should be built, so carpenters need to know about such regulations.

Using rulers, framing squares, chalk lines, and other measuring and marking equipment, carpenters lay out how the work will be done. Using hand and power tools, they cut and shape wood, plywood, fiberglass, plastic, or other materials. Then they nail, screw, glue, or staple the pieces together. Finally, they use levels, plumb bobs, rulers, and squares to check their work, and they make any necessary adjustments. Sometimes carpenters work with prefabricated units for components such as wall panels or stairs. Installing these is, in many ways, a much less complicated task, because much less layout, cutting, and assembly work is needed.

Carpenters who work outside of the building-construction field may do a variety of installation and maintenance jobs, such as repairing furniture and installing ceiling tiles or exterior siding on buildings. Other carpenters specialize in building, repairing, or modifying ships, wooden boats, wooden railroad trestles, timber framing in mine shafts, woodwork inside railcars, storage tanks and vats, or stage sets in theaters.

REQUIREMENTS

High School
A high school education is not mandatory for a good job as a carpenter, but most contractors and developers prefer applicants with a diploma or a GED. A good high school background for prospective carpenters would include carpentry and woodworking courses as well as other shop classes; applied mathematics; mechanical drawing; and blueprint reading.

Postsecondary Training
As an aspiring carpenter, you can acquire the skills of your trade in various ways, through formal training programs and through informal on-the-job training. Of the different ways to learn, an apprenticeship is considered the best, as it provides a more thorough and complete foundation for a career as a carpenter than do other kinds of training. However, the limited number of available apprenticeships means that not all carpenters can learn the trade this way.

A carpenter nails rafters with a nail gun. *(Kevin Leigh/Index Stock Imagery)*

You can pick up skills informally on the job while you work as a carpenter's helper—and many carpenters enter the field this way. You will begin with little or no training and gradually learn as you work under the supervision of experienced carpenters. The skills that you will develop as a helper will depend on the jobs that your employers contract to do. Working for a small contracting company, a beginner may learn about relatively few kinds of carpentry tasks. On the other hand, a large contracting company may offer a wider variety of learning opportunities. Becoming a skilled carpenter by this method can take much longer than an apprenticeship, and the completeness of the training varies. Some individuals waiting for an apprenticeship to become available work as helpers to gain experience in the field.

Some people first learn about carpentry while serving in the military. Others learn skills in vocational programs offered in trade schools and through correspondence courses. Vocational programs can be very good, especially as a supplement to other practical training. But without additional hands-on instruction, vocational school graduates may not be adequately prepared to get many jobs in the field because some programs do not provide sufficient opportunity for students to practice and perfect their carpentry skills.

Apprenticeships, which will provide you with the most comprehensive training available, usually last four years. They are administered by employer groups and by local chapters of labor unions that organize carpenters. Applicants must meet the specific requirements of local apprenticeship committees. Typically, you must be at least 18 years old, have a high school diploma, and be able to show that you have some aptitude for carpentry.

Apprenticeships combine on-the-job work experience with class-room instruction in a planned, systematic program. Initially, you will work at such simple tasks as building concrete forms, doing rough framing, and nailing subflooring. Toward the end of your training, you may work on finishing trimwork, fitting hardware, hanging doors, and building stairs. In the course of this experience, you'll become familiar with the tools, materials, techniques, and equipment of the trade, and you'll learn how to do layout, framing, finishing, and other basic carpentry jobs.

The work-experience segment of an apprenticeship is supple-mented by about 144 hours of classroom instruction per year. Some of this instruction concerns the correct use and maintenance of tools, safety practices, first aid, building-code requirements, and the properties of different construction materials. Other subjects you'll study include the principles of layout, blueprint reading, shop mathematics, and sketching. Both on the job and in the classroom, you'll learn how to work effectively with members of other skilled building trades.

Certification or Licensing
The United Brotherhood of Carpenters and Joiners of America (UBCJA), the national union for the industry, offers certification courses in a variety of specialty skills. These courses teach the ins and outs of advanced skills—like scaffold construction—that help to ensure worker safety while at the same time giving workers ways to enhance their abilities and thus qualify for better jobs. Some job sites require all workers to undergo training in safety techniques and guidelines specified by the Occupational Safety and Health Administration. Workers who have not passed these courses are considered ineligible for jobs at these sites.

Other Requirements
In general, as a carpenter, you'll need to have manual dexterity, good hand-eye coordination, and a good sense of balance. You'll need to be in good physical condition, as the work involves a great deal of physical activity. Stamina is much more important than physical strength. On the job, you may have to climb, stoop, kneel, crouch, and reach as well as deal with the challenges of weather.

EXPLORING

Beyond classes such as woodshop or mechanical drawing, there are a number of real-world ways to begin exploring a career in carpentry and the construction trades. Contact trade organizations such as the National Association of Home Builders or the Associated General Contractors of America; both sponsor student chapters around the country. Consider volunteering for an organization such as Habitat for Humanity; their Youth Programs accept volunteers between the ages of five and 25, and their group-building projects provide hands-on experience. If your school has a drama department, look into it—building sets can be a fun way to learn simple carpentry skills. In addition, your local home improvement store is likely to sponsor classes that teach a variety of skills useful around the house; some of these will focus on carpentry.

A less direct but equally useful method of exploring carpentry is via television. PBS and some cable stations show how-to programs—such as *This Old House* and *New Yankee Workshop*—that feature the work of carpenters.

EMPLOYERS

Carpenters account for a large group of workers in the building trades, holding approximately 1.3 million jobs. About one-third of carpenters work for general-building contractors, and one-fifth work for specialty contractors. About 33 percent are self-employed.

Some carpenters work for manufacturing firms, government agencies, retail and wholesale establishments, or schools. Others work in the shipbuilding, aircraft, or railroad industries. Still others work in the arts, for theaters and movie and television production companies as set builders, or for museums or art galleries, building exhibits.

STARTING OUT

Information about available apprenticeships can be obtained by contacting the local office of the state employment service, area contractors that hire carpenters, or the local offices of the United Brotherhood of Carpenters, which cooperates in sponsoring apprenticeship programs. Helper jobs that can be filled by beginners without special training in carpentry may be advertised in newspaper classified ads or with the state employment service. You might also consider contacting potential employers directly.

ADVANCEMENT

Once an applicant has completed and met all the requirements of apprenticeship training, he or she will be considered a journeyman carpenter. With sufficient experience, journeymen may be promoted to positions responsible for supervising the work of other carpenters. If a carpenter's background includes exposure to a broad range of construction activities, he or she may eventually advance to a position as a general construction supervisor. A carpenter who is skillful at mathematical computations and has a good knowledge of the construction business may become an estimator. An experienced carpenter might one day go into business for himself or herself, doing repair or construction work as an independent contractor.

EARNINGS

According to the U.S. Department of Labor, carpenters had median hourly earnings of $17.11 in 2005. Someone making this wage and working full-time for the year would have an income of approximately $35,580. The lowest-paid 10 percent of carpenters earned less than $10.55 per hour (or approximately $21,940 per year), and the highest-paid 10 percent made more than $29.28 hourly (approximately $60,910 annually). It is important to note, however, that these annual salaries are for full-time work. Many carpenters, like others in the building trades, have periods of unemployment during the year, and their incomes may not match these.

Starting pay for apprentices is approximately 40 percent of the experienced worker's median or roughly $14,200. The wage is increased periodically so that by the fourth year of training apprentice pay is 80 percent of the journeyman carpenter's rate.

Fringe benefits such as health insurance, pension funds, and paid vacations are available to most workers in this field and vary with local union contracts. In general, benefits are more likely to be offered on jobs staffed by union workers.

WORK ENVIRONMENT

Carpenters may work either indoors or outdoors. If they do rough carpentry, they will probably do most of their work outdoors. Carpenters may have to work on high scaffolding or in a basement making cement forms. A construction site can be noisy, dusty, hot, cold, or muddy. Carpenters can expect to be physically active throughout the day, constantly standing, stooping, climbing, and reaching. Some of the possible hazards of the job include being hit by falling objects, falling off scaffolding or a ladder, straining muscles, and getting cuts and scrapes on fingers and hands. Carpenters who follow recommended safety practices and procedures minimize these hazards.

Work in the construction industry involves changing from one job location to another and from time to time being laid off because of poor weather, shortages of materials, or simply lack of jobs. Carpenters must be able to arrange their finances so that they can make it through sometimes long periods of unemployment.

Though it is not required, many carpenters are members of a union such as the UBCJA. Among many other services, such as the certification courses mentioned previously, the union works with employers, seeking to ensure that members receive equitable pay and work in safe conditions.

OUTLOOK

Although the U.S. Department of Labor predicts that employment for carpenters will increase only about as fast as the average through 2014, job opportunities for carpenters are expected to be very strong. This is because replacement carpenters are needed for the large number of experienced carpenters who leave the field every year for work that is less strenuous. Replacement workers are also needed for the fair amount of workers just starting out in the field who decide to move on to other occupations. And, of course, replacements are needed for those who retire. Increased home-building, home modifications for the growing elderly population, two-income couples' desire for larger homes, and the growing population of all ages should contribute to the demand for carpenters.

Factors that will hold down employment growth in the field include the use of more prefabricated building parts and improved tools that make construction easier and faster. In addition, a weak economy has a major impact on the building industry, causing companies and individuals to put off expensive building projects until better times. Carpenters with good all-around skills, such as those who have completed apprenticeships, will have the best job opportunities even in difficult times.

FOR MORE INFORMATION

For information on activities and student chapters, contact
Associated General Contractors of America
2300 Wilson Boulevard, Suite 400
Arlington, VA 22201-5426
Tel: 703-548-3118
Email: info@agc.org
http://www.agc.org

Habitat for Humanity is an internationally recognized nonprofit organization dedicated to the elimination of poverty housing. For information on programs and local chapters found all over the United States, contact
Habitat for Humanity International
121 Habitat Street
Americus, GA 31709-3498
Tel: 229-924-6935, ext. 2551
Email: publicinfo@hfhi.org
http://www.habitat.org

For information on apprenticeships, training programs, and general information about trends in the industry, contact
Home Builders Institute
1201 15th Street, NW, Sixth Floor
Washington, DC 20005-2842
Tel: 800-795-7955
Email: postmaster@hbi.org
http://www.hbi.org

For information about careers in the construction trades and student chapters, contact
National Association of Home Builders
1201 15th Street, NW
Washington, DC 20005-2842
Tel: 800-368-5242
http://www.nahb.com

For information on union membership and apprenticeships, contact
United Brotherhood of Carpenters and Joiners of America
Carpenters Training Fund
6801 Placid Street
Las Vegas, NV 89119-4205
http://www.carpenters.org

Civil Engineers

OVERVIEW

Civil engineers are involved in the design and construction of the physical structures that make up our surroundings, such as roads, bridges, buildings, and harbors. Civil engineering involves theoretical knowledge applied to the practical planning of the layout of our cities, towns, and other communities. It is concerned with modifying the natural environment and building new environments to better the lifestyles of the general public. Civil engineers are also known as *structural engineers*. There are approximately 237,000 civil engineers in the United States.

HISTORY

One might trace the evolution of civil engineering methods by considering the building and many reconstructions of England's London Bridge. In Roman and medieval times, several bridges made of timber were built over the Thames River. Around the end of the 12th century, these were rebuilt into 19 narrow arches mounted on piers. A chapel was built on one of the piers, and two towers were built for defense. A fire damaged the bridge around 1212, yet the surrounding area was considered a preferred place to live and work, largely because it was the only bridge over which one could cross the river. The structure was rebuilt many times during later centuries using different materials and designs. By 1830, it had only five arches. More than a century later, the center span of the bridge was remodeled, and part of it was actually transported to the United States to be set up as a tourist attraction.

QUICK FACTS

School Subjects
Mathematics
Physics

Personal Skills
Leadership/management
Technical/scientific

Work Environment
Indoors and outdoors
Primarily multiple locations

Minimum Education Level
Bachelor's degree

Salary Range
$44,410 to $71,010 to $120,000

Certification or Licensing
Recommended

Outlook
About as fast as the average

DOT
005

GOE
02.07.04

NOC
2131

O*NET-SOC
17-2051.00

Working materials for civil engineers have changed during many centuries. For instance, bridges, once made of timber, then of iron and steel, are today made mainly with concrete that is reinforced with steel. The high strength of the material is necessary because of the abundance of cars and other heavy vehicles that travel over bridges.

As the population continues to grow and communities become more complex, structures that civil engineers must pay attention to have to be remodeled and repaired. New highways, buildings, airstrips, and so forth must be designed to accommodate public needs. Today, more and more civil engineers are involved with water treatment plants, water purification plants, and toxic waste sites. Increasing concern about the natural environment is also evident in the growing number of engineers working on such projects as preservation of wetlands, maintenance of national forests, and restoration of sites around land mines, oil wells, and industrial factories.

THE JOB

Civil engineers use their knowledge of materials science, engineering theory, economics, and demographics to devise, construct, and maintain our physical surroundings. They apply their understanding of other branches of science—such as hydraulics, geology, and physics—to design the optimal blueprint for the project.

Feasibility studies are conducted by *surveying and mapping engineers* to determine the best sites and approaches for construction. They extensively investigate the chosen sites to verify that the ground and other surroundings are amenable to the proposed project. These engineers use sophisticated equipment such as satellites and other electronic instruments to measure the area and conduct underground probes for bedrock and groundwater. They determine the optimal places where explosives should be blasted in order to cut through rock.

Many civil engineers work strictly as consultants on projects, advising their clients. These consultants usually specialize in one area of the industry, such as water systems, transportation systems, or housing structures. Clients include individuals, corporations, and the government. Consultants will devise an overall design for the proposed project, perhaps a nuclear power plant commissioned by an electric company. They will estimate the cost of constructing the plant, supervise the feasibility studies and site investigations, and advise the client on whom to hire for the actual labor involved. Consultants are also responsible for such details as accuracy of drawings and quantities of materials to order.

Other civil engineers work mainly as contractors and are responsible for the actual building of the structure; they are known as *construction engineers*. They interpret the consultants' designs and follow through with the best methods for getting the work done, usually working directly at the construction site. Contractors are responsible for scheduling the work, buying the materials, maintaining surveys of the progress of the work, and choosing the machines and other equipment used for construction. During construction, these civil engineers must supervise the labor and make sure the work is completed correctly and efficiently. After the project is finished, they must set up a maintenance schedule and periodically check the structure for a certain length of time. Later, the task of ongoing maintenance and repair is often transferred to local engineers.

Civil engineers may be known by their area of specialization. *Transportation engineers*, for example, are concerned mainly with the construction of highways and mass transit systems, such as subways and commuter rail lines. When devising plans for subways, engineers are responsible for considering the tunneling involved. *Pipeline engineers* are specialized civil engineers who are involved with the movement of water, oil, and gas through miles of pipeline.

REQUIREMENTS

High School

Because a bachelor's degree is considered essential in the field, high school students interested in civil engineering must follow a college prep curriculum. Students should focus on mathematics (algebra, trigonometry, geometry, and calculus), the sciences (physics and chemistry), computer science, and English and the humanities (history, economics, and sociology). Students should also aim for honors-level courses.

Postsecondary Training

In addition to completing the core engineering curriculum (including mathematics, science, drafting, and computer applications), students can choose their specialty from the following types of courses: structural analysis; materials design and specification; geology; hydraulics; surveying and design graphics; soil mechanics; and oceanography. Bachelor's degrees can be achieved through a number of programs: a four- or five-year accredited college or university; two years in a community college engineering program, plus two or three years in a college or university; or five or six years in a co-op program (attending classes for part of the year and working in an engineering-related job for the rest of the year). About 30 percent of civil engineering students go on to receive a master's degree.

Certification or Licensing

Most civil engineers go on to study and qualify for a professional engineer (P.E.) license. It is required before one can work on projects affecting property, health, or life. Because many engineering jobs are found in government specialties, most engineers take the necessary steps to obtain the license. Requirements are different for each state—they involve educational, practical, and teaching experience. Applicants must take an examination on a specified date.

Other Requirements

Basic personal characteristics often found in civil engineers are an avid curiosity; a passion for mathematics and science; an aptitude for problem solving, both alone and with a team; and an ability to visualize multidimensional, spatial relationships.

EXPLORING

High school students can become involved in civil engineering by attending a summer camp or study program in the field. For example,

Learn More About It

Baine, Celeste. *Is There an Engineer Inside You?: A Comprehensive Guide to Career Decisions in Engineering.* Belmont, Calif.: Professional Publications, 2004.

Blockley, David. *The New Penguin Dictionary of Civil Engineering.* New York: Penguin Books Ltd., 2005.

Chen, Wai-Fa, and J.Y. Richard Liew (eds.). *The Civil Engineering Handbook.* 2nd ed. Boca Raton, Fla.: CRC Press, 2002.

Lewis, Tom. *Divided Highways: Building the Interstate Highways, Transforming American Life.* New York: Penguin Books, 1999.

Lindeburg, Michael R. *101 Solved Civil Engineering Problems.* 4th ed. Belmont, Calif.: Professional Publications, 2001.

Ricketts, Jonathan T., M. Kent Loftin, and Frederick S. Merritt. *Standard Handbook for Civil Engineers.* 5th ed. New York: McGraw-Hill Professional, 2003.

Walesh, Stuart G. *Engineering Your Future: The Non-Technical Side of Professional Practice in Engineering and Other Technical Fields.* 2nd ed. Reston, Va.: American Society of Civil Engineers, 2000.

the Worcester Polytechnic Institute in Massachusetts has a summer program for high school students who have completed their junior year and will be entering their senior year in the fall. Studies and events focus on science and math and include specialties for those interested in civil engineering.

After high school, another way to learn about civil engineering duties is to work on a construction crew involved in the actual building of a project designed and supervised by engineers. Such hands-on experience would provide an opportunity to work near many types of civil workers. Try to work on highway crews or even in housing construction.

EMPLOYERS

Nearly half of all civil engineers work for companies involved in architectural and engineering consulting services. Others work for government agencies at the local, state, or federal level. A small percentage are self-employed, running their own consulting businesses. Approximately 237,000 civil engineers work in the United States.

STARTING OUT

To establish a career as a civil engineer, one must first receive a bachelor's degree in engineering or another appropriate scientific field. College career services offices are often the best sources of employment for beginning engineers. Entry-level jobs usually involve routine work, often as a member of a supervised team. After a year or more (depending on job performance and qualifications), one becomes a junior engineer, then an assistant to perhaps one or more supervising engineers. Establishment as a professional engineer comes after passing the P.E. exam.

ADVANCEMENT

Professional engineers with many years' experience often join with partners to establish their own firms in design, consulting, or contracting. Some leave long-held positions to be assigned as top executives in industries such as manufacturing and business consulting. Also, there are those who return to academia to teach high school or college students. For all of these potential opportunities, it is necessary to keep abreast of engineering advancements and trends by reading industry journals and taking courses.

EARNINGS

Civil engineers are among the lowest paid in the engineering field; however, their salaries are high when compared to those of many other occupations. The mean annual earnings for civil engineers employed in architectural and engineering services were $66,190 in 2005, according to the U.S. Department of Labor. The lowest-paid 10 percent of all civil engineers made less than $44,410 per year, and, at the other end of the pay scale, 10 percent earned more than $100,040 annually. Civil engineers working for the federal government had a mean salary of $77,230 in 2005. According to a 2005 survey by the National Association of Colleges and Employers, starting salaries by degree level averaged as follows: bachelor's, $43,679; master's, $48,050; and doctorate, $59,625. As with all occupations, salaries are higher for those with more experience. Top civil engineers earn as much as $120,000 a year.

Benefits typically include extras such as health insurance, retirement plans, and paid vacation days.

WORK ENVIRONMENT

Many civil engineers work regular 40-hour weeks, often in or near major industrial and commercial areas. Sometimes they are assigned to work in remote areas and foreign countries. Because of the diversity of civil engineering positions, working conditions vary widely. Offices, labs, factories, and actual sites are typical environments for engineers.

A typical work cycle involving various types of civil engineers involves three stages: planning, constructing, and maintaining. Those involved with development of a campus compound, for example, would first need to work in their offices developing plans for a survey. Surveying and mapping engineers would have to visit the proposed site to take measurements and perhaps shoot aerial photographs. The measurements and photos would have to be converted into drawings and blueprints. Geotechnical engineers would dig wells at the site and take core samples from the ground. If toxic waste or unexpected water is found at the site, the contractor determines what should be done.

Actual construction then begins. Very often, a field trailer on the site becomes the engineers' makeshift offices. The campus might take several years to build—it is not uncommon for engineers to be involved in long-term projects. If contractors anticipate that deadlines will not be met, they often put in weeks of 10- to 15-hour days on the job.

After construction is complete, engineers spend less and less time at the site. Some may be assigned to stay on-site to keep daily surveys of how the structure is holding up and to solve problems when they arise. Eventually, the project engineers finish the job and move on to another long-term assignment.

OUTLOOK

Through 2014 employment for civil engineers is expected to grow about as fast as the average, according to the U.S. Department of Labor. Employment will come from the need to maintain and repair public works, such as highways, bridges, and water systems. In addition, as the population grows, so does the need for more transportation and pollution control systems, which creates jobs for those who construct these systems. Firms providing management consulting and computer services may also be sources of jobs for civil engineers. However, employment is affected by several factors, including decisions made by the government to spend further on renewing and adding to the country's basic infrastructure and the health of the economy in general.

FOR MORE INFORMATION

For information on training and scholarships and to read Career Paths in Civil Engineering, visit the society's Web site:
American Society of Civil Engineers
1801 Alexander Bell Drive
Reston, VA 20191-4400
Tel: 800-548-2723
http://www.asce.org

Frontiers is a program for high school seniors that covers science material not traditionally offered in high school. For information, contact
Frontiers
Worcester Polytechnic Institute
100 Institute Road
Worcester, MA 01609-2280
Tel: 508-831-5286
Email: frontiers@wpi.edu
http://www.wpi.edu/Admin/AO/Frontiers

For information on careers and colleges and universities with ITE student chapters, contact

Institute of Transportation Engineers (ITE)
1099 14th Street, NW, Suite 300 West
Washington, DC 20005-3438
Tel: 202-289-0222
Email: ite_staff@ite.org
http://www.ite.org

The JETS offers high school students the opportunity to try engineering through a number of programs and competitions. To find out more about these opportunities or for general career information, contact

Junior Engineering Technical Society
1420 King Street, Suite 405
Alexandria, VA 22314-2794
Tel: 703-548-5387
Email: info@jets.org
http://www.jets.org

College Professors, Architecture

OVERVIEW

College architecture professors teach undergraduate and graduate students about architecture and related subjects at colleges and universities. They are responsible for lecturing classes, leading small seminar groups, and creating and grading examinations. They also may conduct research, write for publication, and aid in administration. Approximately 6,100 postsecondary architecture teachers are employed in the United States.

HISTORY

The concept of colleges and universities goes back many centuries. These institutions evolved slowly from monastery schools, which trained a select few for certain professions. The terms *college* and *university* have become virtually interchangeable in America outside the walls of academia, although originally they designated two very different kinds of institutions.

In 1814, Thomas Jefferson, himself a noted architect, lobbied the University of Virginia to establish architecture as a professional course of study. His efforts were unsuccessful. Not until 1865 was the first formal architecture course taught at the Massachusetts Institute of Technology. The University of Illinois and Cornell University soon followed with their own architectural curricula.

In the 19th century, the Ecole des Beaux-Arts in Paris was considered by many the best architectural school in the world. In fact, many universities and colleges scrambled to have at least one Beaux-Arts professor on staff. The Beaux-Arts method of teaching relied on "learning by doing," and stressed the neoclassical style of architecture. Beaux-Arts professors held many competitions, which were judged by a jury of teachers and guest architects. Many famous American architects, such as Richard Morris Hunt and Charles Follen McKim, were Beaux-Arts alumnae.

By the 20th century, the study of architecture in the United States grew in popularity and became less influenced by the styles of Europe. Architecture professors taught modern architectural concepts, including Frank Lloyd Wright's "Prairie School" style. Students were also given the opportunity to work with materials in class and participate in fieldwork on buildings under construction.

Today, more than 110 architecture programs are accredited by the National Architectural Accrediting Board. In addition, architecture professors teach at about 100 schools that offer a one- or two-year programs concentrating on architectural studies or related technology.

THE JOB

College and university faculty members teach architecture or related courses at junior colleges or at four-year colleges and universities. At four-year institutions, most faculty members are assistant professors, associate professors, or full professors. These three types of professorships differ in regard to status, job responsibility, and salary. Assistant professors are new faculty members working to get tenure (status as a permanent professor); they seek to advance to associate and then to full professorships.

Architecture professors perform three main functions: teaching, advising, and research. Their most important responsibility is to teach students. Their role within a college department will determine the level of courses they teach and the number of courses per semester. Most professors work with students at all levels, from college freshmen to graduate students. They may head several classes a semester or only a few a year. Some of their classes will have large enrollment, while graduate seminars may consist of only 12 or fewer students. Though architecture professors may spend fewer than 10 hours a week in the actual classroom, they spend many hours preparing lectures and lesson plans, grading papers and exams, and preparing grade reports. They also schedule office hours during the week to be available to students outside of the lecture hall, and they meet with students individually throughout the semester.

Many professors teaching this discipline also work in the field as self-employed architects or as members of architectural firms.

In the classroom, professors lecture on such topics as landscape architecture, interior architecture, and historical preservation, as well as teach more advanced classes such as Building Systems, Sustainable Design, Architectural Law, and Housing and Environmental Design. They may lead discussions on the history of architecture, advances in modern designs, and other topics; administer exams; and assign textbook reading and other research. They may also be responsible for mounting departmental exhibitions or galleries. Some professors may be assigned to maintain the department's collection of images to be used for presentations or the department's Web site.

Another important responsibility is advising students. Not all faculty members serve as advisers, but those who do must set aside large blocks of time to guide students through the program. Architecture professors who serve as advisers may have any number of students assigned to them, from fewer than 10 to more than 100, depending on the administrative policies of the college. Their responsibilities may involve looking over a planned program of studies to make sure students meet requirements for graduation or working intensively with each student on many aspects of college life. Some may also help or advise students with job placement after graduation.

The third responsibility of architecture professors is research and publication. Faculty members heavily involved in research programs sometimes are assigned a smaller teaching load. Architecture professors publish their research findings or designs in various trade journals such as *Architectural Record* and the *Architectural Review*. They may also contribute to local newspapers and magazines as architectural experts and write books based on their research or their knowledge and experience in the field of architecture. College and university teachers write most textbooks used to teach architecture classes.

Some faculty members eventually rise to the position of architectural department chair, where they govern the affairs of an entire department. Department chairs, faculty, and other professional staff members are aided in their myriad duties by graduate assistants, who may help develop teaching materials, conduct research, give examinations, teach lower-level courses, and carry out other activities.

Some architecture professors may also conduct classes in an extension program. In such a program, they teach evening and weekend courses for the benefit of people who otherwise would not be able to take advantage of the institution's resources. They may travel away from campus and meet with a group of students at another location.

Typical Classes for Architectural Students

Introduction to Architecture	Integrated Building Systems
History of Architecture	Theories and Methods of
Architectural Theory and	Urban Construction
Criticism	Construction Materials and
Design Fundamentals	Assembly
Computer-Aided Design	Architectural Law
Fundamentals	Ethics and Professional Practice
Site and Landscape Design	Design Studio
Sustainable Design	Architecture Internship

They may work full time for the extension division or may divide their time between on-campus and off-campus teaching.

Distance learning programs, an increasingly popular option for students, give professors the opportunity to use today's technologies to remain in one place while teaching students who are at a variety of locations simultaneously. The professor's duties, like those when teaching correspondence courses conducted by mail, include grading work that students send in at periodic intervals and advising students of their progress. Computers, the Internet, e-mail, and video conferencing, however, are some of the technology tools that allow architecture professors and students to communicate in "real time" in a virtual classroom setting. Meetings may be scheduled during the same time as traditional classes or during evenings and weekends. Professors who do this work are sometimes known as *extension work, correspondence,* or *distance learning instructors.* They may teach online courses in addition to other classes or may have distance learning as their major teaching responsibility.

The *junior college architecture instructor* has many of the same kinds of responsibilities as a teacher in a four-year college or university. Because junior colleges offer only two-year programs, they teach only undergraduates.

REQUIREMENTS

High School

Your high school's college preparatory program likely includes courses in English, foreign language, history, mathematics, physics, and government. In addition, you should take courses in speech to get a sense of what it will be like to lecture to a group of students. Your school's debate team can also help you develop public speaking skills, along with research skills.

Postsecondary Training

Most schools of architecture offer degrees through either a five-year bachelor's program, a three- or four-year master's program, or a two-year master of architecture program for students who have earned a preprofessional undergraduate degree in architecture or a related area. Visit http://www.naab.org for information on accredited programs.

At least one advanced degree in architecture is required to be a professor in a college or university. The master's degree is considered the minimum standard, and graduate work beyond the master's is usually desirable. If you hope to advance in academic rank above instructor, most institutions require a doctorate.

In the last year of your undergraduate program, you'll apply to graduate programs in your area of study. Standards for admission to a graduate program can be high and the competition heavy, depending on the school. Once accepted into a program, your responsibilities will be similar to those of your professors—in addition to attending seminars, you'll research, prepare articles for publication, and teach some undergraduate courses.

You may find employment in a junior college with only a master's degree. Advancement in responsibility and in salary, however, is more likely to come if you have earned a doctorate.

Other Requirements

You should enjoy reading, writing, and researching. Not only will you spend many years studying in school, but your whole career will be based on communicating your thoughts and ideas. People skills are important because you will be dealing directly with students, administrators, and other faculty members on a daily basis. You should feel comfortable in a role of authority and possess self-confidence.

EXPLORING

Your high school teachers use many of the same skills as college professors, so talk to your teachers about their careers and their college experiences. You can develop your own teaching experience by volunteering at a community center, working at a daycare center, or working at a summer camp. Also, spend some time on a college campus to get a sense of the environment. Write to colleges for their admissions brochures and course catalogs (or check them out online); read about the architecture faculty members and the courses they teach. Before visiting college campuses, make arrangements to speak to professors who teach courses that interest you. These professors may allow you to sit in on their classes and observe. Also, make appointments with college advisers and with people in the admissions and recruitment offices. If your grades are good enough, you might be able to serve as a teaching assistant during your undergraduate years, which can give you experience leading discussions and grading papers.

EMPLOYERS

Approximately 6,100 postsecondary architecture teachers are employed in the United States. Employment opportunities vary based on area of study and level of education. With a doctorate, a number of publications, and a record of good teaching, professors should find opportunities in universities all across the country. There are more than 3,800 colleges and universities in the United States; hundreds of these schools have architecture departments or offer related courses. Professors teach in undergraduate and graduate programs. The teaching jobs at doctoral institutions are usually better paying and more prestigious. The most sought-after positions are those that offer tenure. Teachers who have only a master's degree will be limited to opportunities with junior colleges, community colleges, and some small private institutions.

STARTING OUT

You should start the process of finding a teaching position while you are in graduate school. The process includes developing a curriculum vitae (a detailed, academic resume), writing for publication, assisting with research, attending conferences, and gaining teaching experience and recommendations. Many students begin applying for teaching positions while finishing their graduate program. For most positions at four-year institutions, you must travel to large conferences where interviews can be arranged with representatives from the universities to which you have applied.

Because of the competition for tenure-track positions, you may have to work for a few years in temporary positions, visiting various schools as an adjunct professor. Some professional associations maintain lists of teaching opportunities in their areas. They may also make lists of applicants available to college administrators looking to fill an available position.

ADVANCEMENT

The normal pattern of advancement is from instructor to assistant professor, to associate professor, to full professor. All four academic ranks are concerned primarily with teaching and research. College faculty members who have an interest in and a talent for administration may be advanced to chair of a department or to dean of their college. A few become college or university presidents or other types of administrators.

The instructor is usually an inexperienced college teacher. He or she may hold a doctorate or may have completed all the Ph.D. requirements except for the dissertation. Most colleges look upon the rank of instructor as the period during which the college is trying out the teacher. Instructors usually are advanced to the position of assistant professors within three to four years. Assistant professors are given up to about six years to prove themselves worthy of tenure, and if they do so, they become associate professors. Some professors choose to remain at the associate level. Others strive to become full professors and receive greater status, salary, and responsibilities.

Most colleges have clearly defined promotion policies from rank to rank for faculty members, and many have written statements about the number of years in which instructors and assistant professors may remain in grade. Administrators in many colleges hope to encourage younger faculty members to increase their skills and competencies and thus to qualify for the more demanding positions of associate professor and full professor.

EARNINGS

Earnings vary by the size of the school, by the type of school (public, private, women's only, for example), and by the level of position the professor holds. According to the U.S. Department of Labor, in 2005, the median salary for postsecondary architecture teachers was $62,270, with 10 percent earning $97,120 or more and 10 percent earning $45,620 or less. Architecture teachers employed at four-year colleges and universities had mean annual earnings of $67,640; those employed at junior colleges earned $54,610. Those with the highest earnings tend to be senior tenured faculty; those with the lowest, graduate assistants. Professors working on the West

Coast and the East Coast and those working at doctorate-granting institutions also tend to have the highest salaries. Many professors try to increase their earnings by completing research, publishing in their field, or teaching additional courses.

Benefits for full-time faculty typically include health insurance and retirement funds and, in some cases, stipends for travel related to research, housing allowances, and tuition waivers for dependents.

WORK ENVIRONMENT

A college or university is usually a pleasant place to work. Campuses bustle with all types of activities and events, stimulating ideas, and young, energetic populations. Much prestige comes with success as a professor and scholar; professors have the respect of students, colleagues, and others in their community.

Depending on the size of the department, college professors may have their own office, or they may have to share an office with one or more colleagues. Their department may provide them with a computer, Internet access, and research assistants. Architecture professors are also able to do much of their office work at home. They can arrange their schedule around class hours, academic meetings, and the established office hours when they meet with students. Most college teachers work more than 40 hours each week. Although architecture professors may teach only two or three classes a semester, they spend many hours preparing for lectures, examining student work, and conducting research.

OUTLOOK

The U.S. Department of Labor predicts much faster than average employment growth for college and university professors through 2014. College enrollment is projected to grow due to an increased number of 18- to 24-year-olds, an increased number of adults returning to college, and an increased number of foreign-born students. Retirement of current faculty members will also provide job openings. However, competition for full-time, tenure-track positions at four-year schools will be very strong. The U.S. Department of Labor predicts that employment for architects will grow about as fast as the average for all occupations through 2014. The field of architecture is becoming an increasingly popular career option due to its combination of relatively high pay and opportunities for creative individuals. As a result, architecture professors will be needed to train the next generation of architects.

FOR MORE INFORMATION

To read about the issues affecting college professors, contact the following organizations:

American Association of University Professors
1012 14th Street, NW, Suite 500
Washington, DC 20005-3406
Tel: 202-737-5900
Email: aaup@aaup.org
http://www.aaup.org

American Federation of Teachers
555 New Jersey Avenue, NW
Washington, DC 20001-2029
Tel: 202-879-4400
Email: online@aft.org
http://www.aft.org

For information on careers in architecture, visit the following Web site:

Architecture Careers
http://www.archcareers.org

Computer-Aided Design Drafters and Technicians

OVERVIEW

Computer-aided design drafters and technicians, sometimes called *CAD technicians* or *CAD designers,* use computer-based systems to produce or revise technical illustrations needed in the design and development of machines, products, buildings, manufacturing processes, and other work. They use CAD machinery to manipulate and create design concepts so that they are feasible to produce and use in the real world.

HISTORY

Just over 25 years ago, drafting and designing were done with a pencil and paper on a drafting table. To make a circle, drafters used a compass. To draw straight lines and correct angles, they used a straight-edge, T-square, and other tools. With every change required before a design was right, it was "back to the drawing board" to get out the eraser, sharpen the pencil, and revise the drawing. Everybody did it this way, whether the design was simple or complex: automobiles, hammers, printed circuit boards, utility piping, highways, or buildings.

CAD technology came about in the 1970s with the development of microprocessors (computer processors in the form of miniaturized integrated circuits contained on tiny silicon chips). Microprocessors opened up many new uses for computers by greatly reducing the size of computers while also increasing their power and speed.

Interestingly, the drafters and designers working to develop these microprocessors were also the first to benefit from this technology. As the circuits on the silicon chips that the designers were working on became too complex to diagram by pencil and paper, the designers began to use the chips themselves to help store information, create models, and produce diagrams for the design of new chip circuits. This was just the beginning of computer-assisted design and drafting technology. Today, there are tens of thousands of CAD workstations in industrial settings. CAD systems greatly speed up and simplify the designer's and drafter's work. They do more than just let the operator "draw" the technical illustration on the screen. They add the speed and power of computer processing, plus software with technical information that eases the designer/drafter's tasks. CAD systems make complex mathematical calculations, spot problems, offer advice, and provide a wide range of other assistance. Today, nearly all drafting tasks are done with such equipment.

As the Internet has developed, CAD operators can send a CAD drawing across the world in a matter of minutes attached to an e-mail message. Gone are the days of rolling up a print and mailing it. Technology has once again made work more efficient for the CAD designer and drafter.

THE JOB

Technicians specializing in CAD technology usually work in the design and drafting activities associated with new product research and development, although many work in other areas such as structural mechanics or piping. CAD technicians must combine drafting and computer skills. They work in any field where detailed drawings, diagrams, and layouts are important aspects of developing new product designs—for example, in architecture and electronics and in the manufacturing of automobiles, aircraft, computers, and missiles and other defense systems. Most CAD technicians specialize in a particular industry or focus on one part of a design.

CAD technicians work under the direction and supervision of *CAD engineers and designers,* experts highly trained in applying computer technology to industrial design and manufacturing. These designers and engineers plan how to relate CAD technology and equipment to the design process. They are also the ones who give assignments to CAD technicians.

Jackie Sutherland started as a drafter right out of high school, working at a major Midwestern diesel engine manufacturer. Since then, he has moved into a designer's role. In his 25 years on the job, he has seen the transfer from drafting table to CAD workstation.

"I work with everyone from the customer to the engineers, suppliers, pattern makers, and the assembly line from the project concept through the production," says Sutherland of his work as a CAD designer.

Technicians work at specially designed and equipped interactive computer graphics workstations. They call up computer files that hold data about a new product; they then run the programs to convert that information into diagrams and drawings of the product. These are displayed on a video-display screen, which then acts as an electronic drawing board. Following the directions of a CAD engineer or designer, the CAD technician enters changes to the product's design into the computer. The technician merges these changes into the data file and displays the corrected diagrams and drawings.

The software in CAD systems is very helpful to the user—it offers suggestions and advice and even points out errors. The most important advantage of working with a CAD system is that it saves the technician from the lengthy process of having to produce by hand the original and then the revised product drawings and diagrams.

The CAD workstation is equipped to allow technicians to perform calculations, develop simulations, and manipulate and modify the displayed material. Using typed commands at a keyboard, a stylus or light pen for touching the screen display, or a mouse, joystick, or other electronic methods of interacting with the display, technicians can move, rotate, or zoom in on any aspect of the drawing on the screen and project three-dimensional images from two-dimensional sketches. They can make experimental changes to the design and then run tests on the modified design to determine its qualities, such as weight, strength, flexibility, and the cost of required materials. Compared to traditional drafting and design techniques, CAD offers virtually unlimited freedom to explore alternatives and in far less time.

When the product design is complete and the necessary information is assembled in the computer files, technicians may store the newly developed data, output it on a printer, transfer it to another computer, or send it directly to another step of the automated testing or manufacturing process.

Once the design is approved for production, CAD technicians may use their computers to assist in making detailed drawings of certain parts of the design. They may also prepare designs and drawings of the tools or equipment (such as molds, cutting tools, and jigs) that must be specially made in order to manufacture the product. As the product moves toward production, technicians, drafters, and designers may work closely with those assembling the product to ensure the same quality found with prototype testing.

CAD technicians must keep records of all of their test procedures and results. They may need to present written reports, tables, or charts to document their test results or other findings. If a particular system, subsystem, or material has not met a testing or production requirement, technicians may be asked to suggest a way to rearrange the system's components or substitute alternate materials.

The company Sutherland works for also uses interoffice and Internet e-mail to communicate with coworkers and the outside world. "I can attach text, a spreadsheet, or a complete three-dimensional CAD model to a message and send it out to several people through a distribution list. It really shortens the cycle of time on a project," he says.

REQUIREMENTS

High School

CAD technicians must be able to read and understand complex engineering diagrams and drawings. The minimum educational requirement for CAD technicians is a high school diploma. If you are a high school student, take courses that provide you with a solid background in algebra, geometry, trigonometry, physics, machine-shop skills, drafting, and electronics, and take whatever computer courses are available. You should also take courses in English, especially those that improve your communication skills.

Postsecondary Training

Increasingly, most prospective CAD technicians are undertaking formal training beyond the high school level, either through a two-year associate's degree program at a technical school or community college or through a four-year college or university program. Employers prefer job applicants who have some form of postsecondary training in drafting.

Such a program should include courses in these areas: basic drafting, machine drawing, architecture, civil drafting (with an emphasis on highways), process piping, electrical, electrical instrumentation, HVAC, and plumbing. There should also be courses in data processing; computer programming, systems, and equipment, especially video-display equipment; computer graphics; product design; and computer peripheral equipment and data storage. Some two-year programs may also require you to complete courses in technical writing, communications, social sciences, and the humanities.

In addition, some companies have their own training programs, which can last as long as two years. Requirements for entry into these company-run training programs vary from company to company.

If you are considering a career in CAD technology, it is important to remember that you will be required to take continuing education courses even after you have found a job. Continuing education is necessary because technicians need to know about recent advances in technology that may affect procedures, equipment, terminology, or programming concepts.

"Technology changes so fast in this area," says Jackie Sutherland of his many years in the drafting and designing field.

Certification or Licensing

Certification for CAD technicians is voluntary. Certification in drafting is available from the American Design Drafting Association. The test, called the Drafter Certification Examination, covers basic drafting skills but does not include testing of CAD drafting. Applicants are tested on geometric construction, architectural terms and regulations, and working sketches.

Licensing requirements vary. Licensing may be required for specific projects, such as a construction project, when the client requires it.

Other Requirements

As a CAD technician or drafter, you will need to think logically, have good analytical skills, and be methodical, accurate, and detail oriented in all your work. You should be able to work as part of a team as well as independently, since you will spend long periods of time in front of video-display screens.

"You have to be able to visualize what a part may look like or what a new version of a part may look like," says Sutherland. "You have to have basic common sense but also be able to look into the future."

EXPLORING

There are a number of ways to gain firsthand knowledge of the field of CAD technology. Unfortunately, part-time or summer jobs involved directly with CAD technology are very hard to find; however, drafting-related jobs are sometimes available, and many future employers will look favorably on applicants with this kind of experience. In addition, jobs related to other engineering fields, such as electronics or mechanics, may be available and can offer you an opportunity to become familiar with the kind of workplace in which technicians may later be employed.

In addition, high school courses in computers, geometry, physics, mechanical drawing, and shop work will give you a feel for the mental and physical activities associated with CAD technology. Other relevant activities include membership in high school science clubs (especially computer and electronics clubs); participating in science fairs; pursuing hobbies that involve computers, electronics, drafting, mechanical equipment, and model building; and reading books and articles about technical topics.

EMPLOYERS

CAD drafters and technicians are employed in a wide variety of industries, including engineering, architecture, manufacturing, construction, communication, utilities, and the government. They are employed by both large and small companies throughout the United States. For some specialties, jobs may be more specific to certain locations. For example, a drafter or designer for the software industry will find the most opportunities in California's Silicon Valley, while an automotive specialist may be more successful finding jobs near Detroit, Michigan.

STARTING OUT

Probably the most reliable method for entering this field is through your school's career services office. This is especially true for students who graduate from a two-year college or technical institute; recruiters from companies employing CAD technicians sometimes visit such schools, and career services office personnel can help students meet with these recruiters.

As a graduate of a postsecondary program, you can conduct your own job search by contacting architects, building firms, manufacturers, high-technology companies, and government agencies. You can contact prospective employers by phone or e-mail or with a letter stating your interest in employment, accompanied by a resume that provides details about your education and job experience. State or private employment agencies may also be helpful, and classified ads in newspapers, professional journals, and at association Web sites may provide additional leads.

ADVANCEMENT

CAD technicians who demonstrate their ability to handle more responsibility can expect to receive promotions after just a few years on the job. They may be assigned to design work that requires their special skills or experience, such as troubleshooting problems with systems they have worked with, or they may be promoted to supervisory or training positions. As trainers, they may teach courses at their workplace or at a local school or community college.

In general, as CAD technicians advance, their assignments become less and less routine, until they may have a hand in designing and building equipment. Technicians who continue their education and earn a bachelor's degree may become data-processing managers, engineers, systems analysts, or manufacturing analysts.

Other routes for advancement include becoming a sales representative for a design firm or for a company selling computer-aided design services or equipment. It may also be possible to become an independent contractor for companies using or manufacturing CAD equipment.

EARNINGS

Earnings vary among drafters based on the industry they work in as well as their level of experience and the size of their employer. The U.S. Department of Labor reports the median wage for civil and architectural drafters was $40,390 in 2005. The lowest-paid 10 percent of these drafters made less than $26,140 annually; the highest-paid 10 percent made more than $59,590 annually.

According to the 2003 salary survey by the Web site JustCAD-Jobs.com, CAD designers/drafters with two to four years of experience averaged $40,018 annually. Those with four to six years of experience averaged $48,235 per year.

Actual salaries vary widely depending on geographic location, exact job requirements, and the training needed to obtain those jobs. With increased training and experience, technicians can earn higher salaries, and some technicians with special skills, extensive experience, or added responsibilities may earn more.

Benefits usually include health insurance, paid vacations and holidays, pension plans, and sometimes stock-purchase plans.

WORK ENVIRONMENT

CAD professionals almost always work in clean, quiet, well-lighted, air-conditioned offices. CAD technicians spend most of their days at a workstation. While the work does not require great physical effort, it does require patience and the ability to maintain concentration and attention for extended periods of time. Some technicians may find they suffer from eyestrain from working for long periods in front of a computer monitor.

CAD technicians, because of their training and experience, are valuable employees. They are called upon to exercise independent judgment and to be responsible for valuable equipment. Out of necessity, they also sometimes find themselves carrying out routine, uncomplicated tasks. CAD technicians must be able to respond well to both kinds of demands. Most CAD technicians work as part of a team. They are required to follow orders and may encounter situations in which their individual contributions are not fully recognized. Successful CAD technicians are those who work well as team members and who can derive satisfaction from the accomplishments of the team as a whole.

OUTLOOK

The U.S. Department of Labor predicts that the employment outlook for drafters will grow more slowly than average through 2014. The best opportunities will be available to those who have skill and experience using CAD systems. Many companies in the near future will feel pressures to increase productivity in design and manufacturing activities, and CAD technology provides some of the best opportunities to improve that productivity.

Another factor that will create a demand for CAD drafters and technicians is the continued focus on safety and quality throughout manufacturing and industrial fields. In order to do business with leading manufacturers, companies and lower-tier suppliers must meet stringent quality guidelines. With focus on quality as well as safety, companies are scrutinizing their current designs more carefully than ever, requiring more CAD work for new concepts and alterations that will create a better product.

Any economic downturn could adversely affect CAD technicians because many of the industries that they serve—such as auto manufacturing or construction—fluctuate greatly with economic swings. In any event, the best opportunities will be for drafters and technicians proficient in CAD technology who continue to learn, both in school and on the job.

Increasing productivity in the industrial design and manufacturing fields will ensure the long-term economic vitality of our nation;

CAD technology is one of the most promising developments in this search for increased productivity. Knowing that they are in the forefront of this important and challenging undertaking provides CAD technicians and drafters with a good deal of pride and satisfaction.

FOR MORE INFORMATION

For information about certification, student drafting contests, and job postings, contact
American Design Drafting Association
105 East Main Street
Newbern, TN 38059-1526
Tel: 731-627-0802
Email: corporate@adda.org
http://www.adda.org

For information about the electrical field or to find the IEEE-USA student branch nearest you, contact
Institute of Electrical and Electronics Engineers, Inc. (IEEE-USA)
1828 L Street, NW, Suite 1202
Washington, DC 20036-5104
Tel: 202-785-0017
Email: ieeeusa@ieee.org
http://www.ieeeusa.org

For information about scholarships, grants, and student memberships, contact
Society of Manufacturing Engineers
One SME Drive, PO Box 930
Dearborn, MI 48121-0930
Tel: 800-733-4763
http://www.sme.org

Construction Inspectors

OVERVIEW

Construction inspectors work for federal, state, and local governments. Their job is to examine the construction, alteration, or repair of highways, streets, sewer and water systems, dams, bridges, buildings, and other structures to ensure that they comply with building codes and ordinances, zoning regulations, and contract specifications. Approximately 94,000 construction and building inspectors work in the United States.

HISTORY

Construction is one of the major industries of the modern world. Public construction includes structures such as public housing projects; schools; hospitals; administrative and service buildings; industrial and military facilities; highways; and sewer and water systems.

To ensure the public safety of these structures and systems, various governing bodies establish building codes that contractors must follow. The job of the construction inspector is to ensure that the codes are properly followed.

THE JOB

This occupation is made up of four broad categories of specialization: building, electrical, mechanical, and public works.

Building inspectors examine the structural quality of buildings. They check the plans before construction, visit the work site a number of times during construction, and make a final inspection when the project is completed. Some building inspectors specialize in areas such as structural steel or reinforced concrete buildings.

Electrical inspectors visit work sites to inspect the installation of electrical systems and equipment. They check wiring, lighting, generators, and sound and security systems. They may also inspect the wiring for elevators, heating and air-conditioning systems, kitchen appliances, and other electrical installations.

Mechanical inspectors inspect plumbing systems and the mechanical components of heating and air-conditioning equipment and kitchen appliances. They also examine gas tanks, piping, and gas-fired appliances. Some mechanical inspectors specialize in elevators, plumbing, or boilers.

Elevator inspectors inspect both the mechanical and electrical features of lifting and conveying devices such as elevators, escalators, and moving sidewalks. They also test their speed, load allowances, brakes, and safety devices.

Plumbing inspectors inspect plumbing installations, water supply systems, drainage and sewer systems, water heater installations, fire sprinkler systems, and air and gas piping systems; they also examine building sites for soil type to determine water table level, seepage rate, and similar conditions.

Heating and refrigeration inspectors examine heating, ventilating, air-conditioning, and refrigeration installations in new buildings and approve alteration plans for those elements in existing buildings.

Public works inspectors make sure that government construction of water and sewer systems, highways, streets, bridges, and dams conforms to contract specifications. They visit work sites to inspect excavations, mixing and pouring of concrete, and asphalt paving. They also keep records of the amount of work performed and the materials used so that proper payment can be made. These inspectors may specialize in highways, reinforced concrete, or ditches.

Construction inspectors use measuring devices and other test equipment, take photographs, keep a daily log of their work, and write reports. If any detail of a project does not comply with the various codes, ordinances, or specifications, or if construction is being done without proper permits, the inspectors have the authority to issue a stop-work order.

REQUIREMENTS
High School
People interested in becoming construction inspectors must be high school graduates who have taken courses in drafting, algebra, geometry, and English. Additional shop courses will undoubtedly prove helpful as well.

Postsecondary Training

Most employers prefer graduates of an apprenticeship program, community or junior college, or people with at least two years toward an engineering or architectural degree. Required courses include construction technology, blueprint reading, technical math, English, and building inspection.

Most construction inspectors have several years' experience either as a construction contractor or supervisor or as a craft or trade worker such as a carpenter, electrician, plumber, or pipefitter. This experience demonstrates knowledge of construction materials and practices, which is necessary in inspections. Construction inspectors receive most of their training on the job.

Certification or Licensing

Some states require certification for employment. Inspectors can earn a certificate by passing examinations on construction techniques, materials, and code requirements. The exams are offered by the International Code Council.

Other Requirements

A construction inspector should have experience in construction, have a good driving record, be in good physical shape, have good communication skills, be able to pay attention to details, and have a strong personality. Although there are no standard requirements to enter this occupation, an inspector should be a responsible individual with in-depth knowledge of the construction trades. Inexperience can lead to mistakes that can cost someone a staggering amount of money or even cause a person's death.

The trade is not considered hazardous, but most inspectors wear hard hats as a precaution. Inspectors might need to climb ladders and walk across rooftops or perhaps trudge up numerous flights of stairs at building projects where elevators are not yet installed. Or they might occasionally find themselves squirming through the dirty, narrow, spider-infested crawl space under a house to check a foundation or crawling across the joists in a cramped, dusty, unfinished attic, inhaling insulation fibers and pesticides.

After the inspection, a construction inspector needs to explain his or her findings clearly in reports and should expect to spend many hours answering questions in person, by telephone, and in letters. Because they often deliver bad news, they also need the emotional strength to stand firm on their reports, even when someone calls them a liar or threatens to sue.

On the other hand, inspectors know that the purpose of their work is to protect people. For example, they help ensure that a couple's new house will not be apt to burn down from an electrical short, and they might point out less dangerous problems, such as a malfunctioning septic tank or a leaking roof, that could require expensive repairs.

EXPLORING

Field trips to construction sites and interviews with contractors or building trade officials are good ways to gain practical information about what it is like to work in the industry and how best to prepare for it. Summer jobs at a construction site provide an overview of the work involved in a building project. Students may also seek part-time jobs with a general contracting company, with a specialized contractor (such as a plumbing or electrical contractor), or as a carpenter's helper. Jobs in certain supply houses will help students become familiar with construction materials.

EMPLOYERS

Approximately 94,000 construction and building inspectors are employed in the United States. Approximately 45 percent work for local governments, such as municipal or county building departments. Another 25 percent work for architecture or engineering firms. Inspectors employed at the federal level work for such agencies as the Department of Defense or the departments of Housing and Urban Development, Agriculture, and the Interior.

STARTING OUT

People without postsecondary education usually enter the construction industry as a trainee or apprentice. Graduates of technical schools or colleges of construction and engineering can expect to start work as an engineering aide, drafter, estimator, or assistant engineer. Jobs may be found through school career services offices, employment agencies, and unions or by applying directly to contracting company personnel offices. Application may also be made directly to the employment offices of the federal, state, or local governments.

ADVANCEMENT

The federal, state, and large city governments provide formal training programs for their construction inspectors to keep them abreast of new building-code developments and to broaden their knowledge of construction materials, practices, and inspection techniques. Inspectors for small agencies can upgrade their skills by attending state-conducted training programs or taking college or correspondence courses. An engineering degree is usually required to become a supervisory inspector.

EARNINGS

The U.S. Department of Labor reports that the median annual income for construction and building inspectors was $44,720 in 2005. The lowest-paid 10 percent of these workers had annual earnings of less than $28,390; the highest-paid 10 percent made more than $69,650. Inspectors employed by architectural and engineering services had mean annual earnings of $47,710. Earnings vary based on the inspector's experience, the type of employer, and the location of the work. Salaries are slightly higher in the North and West than in the South and are considerably higher in large metropolitan areas. Building inspectors earn slightly more than other inspectors.

WORK ENVIRONMENT

Construction inspectors work both indoors and outdoors, dividing their time between their offices and the work sites. Inspection sites

Mean Annual Earnings for Construction Inspectors By Industry, 2005

Federal government:	$73,310
Insurance carriers:	$65,040
Power generation and supply:	$57,260
Management of companies and enterprises:	$55,330
Management and technical consulting services:	$51,500
Nonresidential building construction:	$50,220
Architectural and engineering services:	$47,710
Local government:	$46,650
State government:	$41,390

Source: U.S. Department of Labor

are dirty and cluttered with tools, machinery, and debris. Although the work is not considered hazardous, inspectors must climb ladders and stairs and crawl under buildings.

The hours are usually regular, but when there is an accident at a site, the inspector has to remain on the job until reports have been completed. The work is steady year-round, rather than seasonal, as are some other construction occupations. In slow construction periods, inspectors are kept busy examining the renovation of older buildings.

OUTLOOK

As the concern for public safety continues to rise, the demand for inspectors should grow faster than the average through 2014 even if construction activity does not increase. The level of new construction fluctuates with the economy, but maintenance and renovation continue during the downswings, so inspectors are rarely laid off. Applicants who have some college education, are already certified inspectors, or who have experience as carpenters, electricians, or plumbers will have the best opportunities. Construction and building inspectors tend to be older, more experienced workers who have worked in other construction occupations for many years.

FOR MORE INFORMATION

For additional information on a career as a construction inspector, contact

American Construction Inspectors Association
12995 6th Street, Suite 69
Yucaipa, CA 92399-2549
Tel: 888-867-2242
Email: office@acia.com.
http://www.acia.com

American Society of Home Inspectors
932 Lee Street, Suite 101
Des Plaines, IL 60016-6546
Tel: 800-743-2744
http://www.ashi.com

Association of Construction Inspectors
1224 North Nokomis, NE
Alexandria, MN 56308-5072

Tel: 320-763-7525
Email: aci@iami.org
http://www.iami.org/aci.cfm

International Code Council
5203 Leesburg Pike, Suite 600
Falls Church, VA 22041-3401
Tel: 888-422-7233
http://www.iccsafe.org

Construction Managers

QUICK FACTS

School Subjects
Mathematics
Technical/shop

Personal Skills
Leadership/management
Technical/scientific

Work Environment
Indoors and outdoors
Primarily multiple locations

Minimum Education Level
Some postsecondary training

Salary Range
$42,900 to $72,260 to
$136,670+

Certification or Licensing
Recommended

Outlook
About as fast as the average

DOT
N/A

GOE
N/A

NOC
0711

O*NET-SOC
11-9021.00

OVERVIEW

Construction managers, also known as *construction foremen, supervisors,* and *contractors,* oversee the planning and building of residential, commercial, and industrial projects. They may be self-employed or salaried employees for large construction firms and real estate developers. Others may contract their services on a project-by-project basis. There are approximately 431,000 construction managers employed in the United States.

HISTORY

Construction, the building of any structure or infrastructure, has existed since early man found the need to create shelter. Simple huts or cabins evolved to more sturdy structures, dirt paths changed to paved roads, and bridges were built to connect land once separated by rivers or streams.

As construction projects became larger and more complicated, the need arose for someone to organize and manage the many workers involved—the construction manager. In the past, managers came to their position after years of on-the-job experience—as carpenters, masonry workers, electricians, plumbers, or a host of other industry trades. Today, construction managers often have a college degree in construction science or engineering, as well as practical knowledge of the industry.

The growth of the construction industry and the need for qualified workers and managers resulted in the formation of various organizations devoted to training, educating, and advocating for those employed in construction. One such organization is the American Institute of

Constructors (AIC). Founded in 1969, the AIC offers support and a standard of ethics for construction professionals. Members are entitled to continuing education and training, certification, and information on advances in the science of construction management.

THE JOB

The construction of any structure, whether a small bungalow or a skyscraper, is a complicated process. When erecting a new building, for example, an architect must first design the building according to the owner's wishes; carpenters, masonry workers, electricians, and plumbers must work on the foundation, interior, and exterior of the structure; and building inspectors must ensure all work is done according to the city's code. The construction manager is considered the supervisor and liaison for every step of a building's creation.

For smaller projects, such as a house, construction managers may be responsible for the entire project. If the house is to be built as part of a subdivision, they may act as a liaison between the developer and prospective homeowner. Construction managers may be asked to oversee any requested changes to the existing blueprint. They are also responsible for hiring and scheduling the various crews needed for construction—excavation teams to dig out and lay the foundation; carpenters for the frame and woodwork; masonry workers for exterior and interior brickwork; and plumbers, electricians, and any specialized craftspeople needed to complete the project.

Industrial and large commercial projects are more complicated and may warrant more than one construction manager for the task. Assistant managers or foremen are often hired to oversee a particular part or phase of a large project, such as zoning and site preparation or electrical and plumbing. Assistant managers may work with civil engineers on the structure of a new road, or with landscape architects on the renovation of a golf resort. Each assistant manager is responsible for applying for the necessary permits and licenses, as well as meeting with city code officers for periodic and final inspections. If the project does not pass inspection or violates any safety regulations, it is the manager's responsibility to make the needed changes to bring the project to compliance.

Construction managers must know how to work within a specified budget. The inventory of building materials and tools is important. Managers must make sure costly supplies of steel and granite, for example, are not being wasted. They keep track of expensive tools and equipment and make certain they are used properly. If special equipment is needed, such as a state-of-the-art

Two construction managers review blueprints at a construction site.
(Tomas del Amo/Index Stock Imagery)

fire-suppression system, construction managers must be able to procure it at a reasonable price.

The management of a large crew is a very important part of a construction manager's job. Once a qualified team of workers is assembled, their daily work output must be monitored, since it is the responsibility of the manager to make sure that a construction project is completed on schedule. Some managers may take on the responsibility of creating work schedules, calculating wages, or assigning benefits for workers. If there are any work-related issues, such as disagreements between workers, construction managers are called on to settle them. Most important, however, a construction manager is responsible for the safety of the crew and safe and timely completion of the final project.

REQUIREMENTS

High School
If you are thinking about a career in construction management, chances are you have a knack for building things. Industrial arts classes such as woodworking, welding, and drafting and design will give you good background experience for the construction industry.

Construction managers are savvy business professionals as well. Give yourself a solid introduction to the business side of this job by taking classes such as accounting, finance, management, and mathematics.

Postsecondary Training

Many construction managers have an associate's or bachelor's degree in construction science, construction management, or civil engineering. A typical class load for students studying construction science, for example, includes construction methods, building codes, engineering, site planning, and cost estimating. Some even earn their master's degree in these fields. Visit http://www.acce-hq.org for information on accredited programs.

Certification and Licensing

Certification is available from the American Institute of Constructors (AIC) after successful completion of a written examination and verification of relevant work experience. Two designations are offered—associate constructor and certified professional constructor. Examinations cover different specialties of the construction industry, including commercial, industrial, residential, mechanical, and electrical.

The Construction Management Association of America (CMAA) offers the designation of certified construction manager to applicants who pass an examination and meet educational and experience requirements. While AIC and CMAA certification programs are voluntary, many industry professionals chose to become certified, increasing their chances for promotion. Many employers look favorably upon job candidates with certification.

Other Requirements

Construction managers must have a thorough understanding of the construction business ranging from the hands-on side to the managerial. They should be able to understand blueprints and technical drawings and be familiar with the various tools and building materials. Some construction managers may use computer-design programs to help with revising blueprints. Excellent supervisory skills are also needed to keep a project moving according to schedule, while at the same time motivating a crew to perform their best work.

Managers must be good communicators, since they deal with many different types of people throughout the course of a building project, from engineers and city officials to trades people. Managers are often under great pressure to prepare contracts and bid on projects, as well as address any problems that arise during the project. For example, if a preordered amount of steel is short of that needed to finish a structure, construction managers must be able to find more materials quickly but without going beyond the project's budget.

EXPLORING

There are many ways to investigate this industry as a high school student. Why not find a summer part-time job with a local construction company? Don't count on operating the big machines—leave these to the professionals. Rather, you will be given small tasks around the site or assist trades people with their work. Regardless of the work, you can earn valuable experience and learn what the work environment is really like.

You can also manage your own building project, such as a tree house or fort. "Hire" your friends to help you as designers or construction workers. You will be in charge of completing each phase of the project—from designing the structure, setting the budget, ordering supplies, supervising your crew of workers, and building the structure.

EMPLOYERS

Approximately 431,000 construction managers are employed in the United States. More than 50 percent are self-employed. Employment opportunities exist in a variety of settings. Many construction managers work for small construction companies that specialize in residential homes or small commercial projects. They are often in charge of the entire project from start to finish.

Construction managers employed by larger firms, real estate developers, or engineering firms may only be assigned to work on a particular phase of the project, such as the structural framework, or specialize in a certain area such as fireproofing or a specific type of construction such as bridges.

Job availability is nationwide but may be more plentiful in areas experiencing high growth. Managers who wish to work with larger companies and more visible projects may need to relocate to major metropolitan areas.

STARTING OUT

Traditionally, construction managers were promoted into managerial positions after many years of work experience in the construction industry. That is still possible today, though more common in smaller construction firms. Larger construction companies or major developers demand managerial candidates with construction experience as well as a college degree. Jobs can be found via school career services offices, newspaper and Internet job advertisements, employment agencies, and unions or by applying directly to contracting company personnel offices. Professional organizations, such as the Construction Management Association of America, also provide job listings at their Web sites.

ADVANCEMENT

Since construction managers already hold a high-tier position in the construction industry, promotion may be limited, especially with smaller firms. Some construction managers may move to larger companies that deal with bigger building contracts and projects. Promotion within larger companies may take the form of an upper-level management or executive position.

Some construction managers choose to open their own construction firms or branch off into real estate development. Others may choose to continue their education and become architects or engineers.

EARNINGS

Earnings for construction managers vary based on the manager's experience, the type of employer, and the location of the work. The U.S. Department of Labor reports the median annual income for construction managers was $72,260 in 2005. The lowest-paid 10 percent of these workers had annual earnings of less than $42,900; the highest-paid 10 percent made more than $136,670. Construction managers typically receive benefits such as health insurance, paid vacation and sick days, and eligibility for retirement savings plans.

WORK ENVIRONMENT

Construction managers work both indoors and outdoors. They typically work out of a central office but spend a considerable amount of time at job sites. Although this career is not considered hazardous, job sites can be dirty and cluttered with tools, equipment, and construction debris.

Construction managers often travel between job sites—some of which may be located great distances from one another. Some managers get the opportunity to oversee projects in other regions of the United States or even in other countries.

Managers work irregular hours and are often on call 24 hours a day to respond to emergencies and work stoppages due to weather delays or to meet project deadlines.

OUTLOOK

Employment for construction managers is expected to grow about as fast as the average for all occupations through 2014, according to the U.S. Department of Labor. A shortage of qualified workers, the growing complexity and number of construction projects, and the need for better cost management of construction projects have spurred strong demand for construction managers—especially those with experience and bachelor's or higher degrees in construction science, construction management, or civil engineering.

FOR MORE INFORMATION

For industry news, student and full membership information, and certification opportunities, contact
American Institute of Constructors
PO Box 26334
Alexandria, VA 22314-6334
Tel: 703-683-4999

For information on different careers within the construction industry and apprenticeship information, contact
Building and Construction Trades Department
815 16th Street, Suite 600
Washington, DC 20006-4101
Tel: 202-347-1461
http://www.buildingtrades.org

For industry news and certification opportunities, contact
Construction Management Association of America
7918 Jones Branch Drive, Suite 546
McLean, VA 22102-3337
Tel: 703-356-2622
Email: info@cmaanet.org
http://cmaanet.org

To learn more about industry standards, available training programs, and career information, contact
National Center for Construction Education and Research
PO Box 141104
Gainesville, FL 32614-1104
Tel: 888-622-3720
http://www.nccer.org

Cost Estimators

OVERVIEW

Cost estimators use standard estimating techniques to calculate the cost of a construction or manufacturing project. They help contractors, owners, and project planners determine how much a project or product will cost to decide if it is economically viable. There are approximately 198,000 cost estimators employed in the United States.

HISTORY

Cost estimators collect and analyze information on various factors influencing costs, such as the labor, materials, and machinery needed for a particular project. Cost estimating became a profession as production techniques became more complex. Weighing the many costs involved in a construction or manufacturing project soon required specialized knowledge beyond the skills and training of the average builder or contractor. Today, cost estimators work in many industries but are predominantly employed in construction and manufacturing.

THE JOB

In the construction industry, the nature of the work is largely determined by the type and size of the project being estimated. For a large building project, for example, the estimator reviews architectural drawings and other bidding documents before any construction begins. The estimator then visits the potential construction site to collect information that may affect the way the structure is built, such as the site's access to transportation, water, electricity, and other needed resources. While out in the field, the estimator also analyzes the topography of the land, taking note of its general characteristics, such as drainage areas and the location of trees and other vegetation. After compiling thorough research, the estimator writes a quantity survey, or takeoff. This is an itemized report of the quantity of materials and labor a firm will need for the proposed project.

Large projects often require several estimators, all specialists in a given area. For example, one estimator may assess the electrical costs of a project, while another concentrates on the transportation or insurance costs. In this case, it is the responsibility of a *chief estimator* to combine the reports and submit one development proposal.

In manufacturing, estimators work with engineers to review blueprints and other designs. They develop a list of the materials and labor needed for production. Aiming to control costs but maintain quality, estimators must weigh the option of producing parts in-house or purchasing them from other vendors. After this research, they write a report on the overall costs of manufacturing, taking into consideration influences such as improved employee learning curves, material waste, overhead, and the need to correct problems as manufacturing goes along.

To write their reports, estimators must know current prices for labor and materials and other factors that influence costs. They obtain this data through commercial price books, catalogs, and the Internet or by calling vendors directly to obtain quotes.

Estimators should also be able to compute and understand accounting and mathematical formulas in order to make their cost reports. Computer programs are frequently used to do routine calculations, producing more accurate results and leaving the estimator with more time to analyze data.

REQUIREMENTS

High School

To prepare for a job in cost estimating, you should take courses in accounting, business, economics, and mathematics. Because a large part of this job involves comparing calculations, it is essential that you are comfortable and confident with your math skills. English courses with heavy concentration in writing are also recommended to develop your communication skills. Cost estimators must be able to write clear and accurate reports of their analyses. Finally, drafting and shop courses are also useful, since estimators must be able to review and understand blueprints and other design plans.

Postsecondary Training

Though not required for the job, most employers of cost estimators in both construction and manufacturing prefer applicants with formal education. In construction, cost estimators generally have associate's or bachelor's degrees in construction management, construction science, engineering, or architecture. Those employed with manufacturers often have degrees in physical science, business, mathematics, operations research, statistics, engineering, economics, finance, or accounting.

Many colleges and universities offer courses in cost estimating as part of the curriculum for an associate's, bachelor's, or master's degree. These courses cover subjects such as cost estimating, cost control, project planning and management, and computer applications. The Association for the Advancement of Cost Engineering International offers a list of education programs related to cost engineering. Check out the association's Web site, http://www.aacei.org, for more information.

Certification or Licensing

Although it is not required, many cost estimators find it helpful to become certified to improve their standing within the professional community. Obtaining certification proves that the estimator has obtained adequate job training and education. Information on certification procedures is available from organizations such as the American Society of Professional Estimators, the Association for the Advancement of Cost Engineering International, and the Society of Cost Estimating and Analysis.

Other Requirements

To be a cost estimator, you should have sharp mathematical and analytical skills. Cost estimators must work well with others and be confident and assertive when presenting findings to engineers, business owners, and design professionals. To work as a cost estimator in the construction industry, you will likely need some experience before you start, which can be gained through an internship or cooperative education program.

EXPLORING

Practical work experience is necessary to become a cost estimator. Consider taking a part-time position with a construction crew or manufacturing firm during your summer vacations. Because of more favorable working conditions, construction companies are busiest

Tallest Buildings in the World

Building	Country	Height (in feet)
Taipei 101	Taiwan	1,670
Petronas Tower 1	Malaysia	1,483
Petronas Tower 2	Malaysia	1,483
Sears Tower	United States	1,450
Jin Mao Building	China	1,380
Two International Finance Centre	Hong Kong	1,362
CITIC Plaza	China	1,283
Shun Hing Square	China	1,260
Empire State Building	United States	1,250
Central Plaza	Hong Kong	1,227

Source: Infoplease.com

during the summer months and may be looking for additional assistance. Join any business or manufacturing clubs that your school may offer.

Another way to discover more about career opportunities is simply by talking to a professional cost estimator. Ask your school counselor to help arrange an interview with an estimator to ask questions about his or her job demands, work environment, and personal opinion of the job.

EMPLOYERS

Approximately 198,000 cost estimators are employed in the United States: 58 percent by the construction industry and 17 percent by manufacturing companies. Other employers include engineering and architecture firms, business services, the government, and a wide range of other industries.

Estimators are employed throughout the country, but the largest concentrations are found in cities or rapidly growing suburban areas. More job opportunities exist in or near large commercial or government centers.

STARTING OUT

Cost estimators often start out working in the industry as laborers, such as construction workers. After gaining experience and taking the necessary training courses, a worker may move into the more specialized role of estimator. Another possible route into cost estimating is through a formal training program, either through a professional organization that sponsors educational programs or through technical schools, community colleges, or universities. School placement counselors can be good sources of employment leads for recent graduates. Applying directly to manufacturers, construction firms, and government agencies is another way to find your first job.

Whether employed in construction or manufacturing, most cost estimators are provided with intensive on-the-job training. Generally, new hires work with experienced estimators to become familiar with the work involved. They develop skills in blueprint reading and learn construction specifications before accompanying estimators to the construction site. In time, new hires learn how to determine quantities and specifications from project designs and report appropriate material and labor costs.

ADVANCEMENT

Promotions for cost estimators are dependent on skill and experience. Advancement usually comes in the form of more responsibility and higher wages. A skilled cost estimator at a large construction company may become a chief estimator. Some experienced cost estimators go into consulting work, offering their services to government, construction, and manufacturing firms.

EARNINGS

Salaries vary according to the size of the construction or manufacturing firm and the experience and education of the worker. According to the U.S. Department of Labor, the median annual salary for cost estimators was $52,020 in 2005. The lowest 10 percent earned less than $31,200 and the highest 10 percent earned more than $87,040. By industry, the mean annual earnings were as follows: nonresidential building construction, $62,960; building equipment contractors, $58,740; foundation and exterior contractors, $56,280; residential building construction, $55,860; and building finishing contractors, $55,460. Starting salaries for graduates of engineering or construction management programs were higher than those with degrees in other fields. A salary survey by the National Association of Colleges and Employers reports that candidates with degrees in construction science/management were offered average starting salaries of $42,923 in 2005.

WORK ENVIRONMENT

Much of the cost estimator's work takes place in a typical office setting with access to accounting records and other information. However, estimators must also visit construction sites or manufacturing facilities to inspect production procedures. These sites may be dirty, noisy, and potentially hazardous if the cost estimator is not equipped with proper protective gear such as a hard hat or earplugs. During a site visit, cost estimators consult with engineers, work supervisors, and other professionals involved in the production or manufacturing process.

Estimators usually work a 40-hour week, although longer hours may be required if a project faces a deadline. For construction estimators, overtime hours almost always occur in the summer, when most projects are in full force.

OUTLOOK

Employment for cost estimators is expected to increase faster than the average through 2014, according to the U.S. Department of Labor. As in most industries, highly trained college graduates and those with the most experience will have the best job prospects.

Many jobs will arise from the need to replace workers leaving the industry, either to retire or change jobs. In addition, growth within the residential and commercial construction industry is a large cause for much of the employment demand for estimators. The fastest-growing areas in construction are in special trade and government projects, including the building and repairing of highways, streets, bridges, subway systems, airports, water and sewage systems, and electric power plants and transmission lines. Additionally, opportunities will be good in residential and school construction, as well as in the construction of nursing and extended care facilities. Cost estimators with degrees in construction management or in construction science, engineering, or architecture will have the best employment prospects. In manufacturing, employment is predicted to remain stable, though growth is not expected to be as strong as in construction. Estimators will be in demand because employers will continue to need their services to control operating costs. Estimators with degrees in engineering, science, mathematics, business administration, or economics will have the best employment prospects in this industry.

FOR MORE INFORMATION

For information on certification and educational programs, contact
American Society of Professional Estimators
2525 Perimeter Place Drive, Suite 103
Nashville, TN 37214-3674
Tel: 888-EST-MATE
Email: info@aspenational.com
http://www.aspenational.com

For information on certification, educational programs, and scholarships, contact
Association for the Advancement of Cost Engineering International
209 Prairie Avenue, Suite 100
Morgantown, WV 26501-5934
Tel: 800-858-2678
Email: info@aacei.org
http://www.aacei.org

For information on certification, job listings, and a glossary of cost-estimating terms, visit the SCEA Web site:
Society of Cost Estimating and Analysis (SCEA)
101 South Whiting Street, Suite 201
Alexandria, VA 22304-3416
Tel: 703-751-8069
Email: scea@sceaonline.net
http://www.sceaonline.net

Drafters

OVERVIEW

Drafters prepare working plans and detail drawings of products or structures from the rough sketches, specifications, and calculations of engineers, architects, and designers. These drawings are used in engineering or manufacturing processes to reproduce exactly the product or structure desired, according to the specified dimensions. The drafter uses knowledge of various machines, engineering practices, mathematics, and building materials, along with other physical sciences and fairly extensive computer skills, to complete the drawings. There are approximately 254,000 drafters working in the United States.

HISTORY

In industry, drafting is the conversion of ideas from people's minds to precise working specifications from which products can be made. Many people find it much easier to give visual rather than oral or written directions and to assemble new equipment if the instructions include diagrams and drawings. Often, this is especially true in complex situations or when a large number of people are involved; drawings allow all aspects to be addressed and everyone to receive the same information at the same time. Industry has come to rely on drafters to develop the working specifications from the new ideas and findings of people in laboratories, shops, factories, and design studios.

Perspective drawings and photographs are easily interpreted because they closely resemble visual images. Objects appear to decrease in relative size as they recede from the viewer, and the angular relation of their lines and edges is distorted. The lines of sight appear to converge at a single point in the image. Drafting is based on a slightly different method of depiction, called orthographic projection. The projection used for engineering and architectural drawings is called orthogonal (right-angled) or orthographic because the lines of sight from points on the object to the picture plane of the image are perpendicular to that plane. They are parallel, rather than convergent. It's a different way of seeing the relations between the parts of an object.

Orthographic projection is the basis of the branch of mathematics known as descriptive geometry. Although some material appeared earlier, and the general precepts were developed to a much greater degree afterwards, the 1798 publication of the book *Géométrie Descriptive* by French mathematician Gaspard Monge is widely recognized as the first exposition of descriptive geometry and the formalization of orthographic projection. The growth and development of the drafting profession were facilitated by the application of Monge's concepts. The Industrial Revolution and the need it inspired for interchangeable parts, the introduction of the blueprinting process, and the monetary savings to be gained by a carefully calculated set of drawings that made working models less of a necessity all contributed to the advancement of the field.

THE JOB

The drafter prepares detailed plans and specification drawings from the ideas, notes, or rough sketches of scientists, engineers, architects, and designers. Sometimes drawings are developed after a visit to a project in the field or as the result of a discussion with one or more people involved in the job. The drawings, which usually provide a number of different views of the object, must be exact and accurate. They vary greatly in size depending on the type of drawing. Some assembly drawings, often called layouts, are 25 to 30 feet long, while others are very small. Drawings must contain enough detail, whatever their size, so that the part, object, or building can be constructed from them. Such drawings usually include information concerning the quality of materials to be used, their cost, and the processes to be followed in carrying out the job. In developing drawings made to scale of the object to be built, drafters may use a variety of instruments, such as protractors, compasses, triangles, squares, drawing pens, and pencils. Most drafters, however, now use computers or computer-aided design and drafting (CAD or CADD) systems.

Drafters often are classified according to the type of work they do or their level of responsibility. *Senior drafters* use the preliminary information and ideas provided by engineers and architects to make design layouts. They may have the title of *chief drafter*, and so assign work to other drafters and supervise their activities. *Detailers* make complete drawings, giving dimensions, material, and any other necessary information of each part shown on the layout. *Checkers* carefully examine drawings to check for errors in computing or in recording dimensions and specifications. *Tracers*, who are usually assistant drafters, make corrections and prepare drawings for reproduction by tracing them on transparent cloth, paper, or plastic film.

Drafters also may specialize in a particular field of work, such as mechanical, electrical, electronic, aeronautical, structural, or architectural drafting. Although the nature of the work of drafters is not too different from one specialization to another, there is considerable variation in the type of object with which they deal. The following paragraphs detail specialties in the architectural and building industries.

Commercial drafters do all-around drafting, such as plans for building sites, layouts of offices and factories, and drawings of charts, forms, and records. *Computer-assisted drafters* within this specialty use computers to make drawings and layouts for such fields as aeronautics, architecture, or electronics.

Civil drafters make construction drawings for roads and highways, river and harbor improvements, flood control, drainage, and other civil engineering projects. *Structural drafters* draw plans for bridge trusses, plate girders, roof trusses, trestle bridges, and other structures that use structural reinforcing steel, concrete, masonry, and other structural materials.

Cartographic drafters prepare maps of geographic areas to show natural and constructed features, political boundaries, and other features. Topographical drafters draft and correct maps from original sources, such as other maps, surveying notes, and aerial photographs. *Architectural drafters* draw plans of buildings, including artistic and structural features. *Landscape drafters* make detailed drawings from sketches furnished by landscape architects.

Heating and ventilating drafters draft plans for heating, air-conditioning, ventilating, and sometimes refrigeration equipment. *Plumbing drafters* draw diagrams for the installation of plumbing equipment. *Mechanical drafters* make working drawings of machinery, automobiles, power plants, or any mechanical device. *Electrical drafters* make schematics and wiring diagrams to be used by construction crews working on equipment and wiring in power plants, communications centers, buildings, or electrical distribution systems. Other types of drafters include aeronautical drafters; automotive design drafters and automotive design layout drafters; castings drafters; directional survey drafters; electromechanical drafters; electromechanisms design drafters; electronics drafters; geological drafters; geophysical drafters; marine drafters; oil and gas drafters; patent drafters; and tool design drafters.

No matter their specialty, drafters increasingly have come to rely on the use of computers in their work. Early programs were first developed in the 1960s to assist in the composition of graphic images on screen, to retain and then retrieve the associated data in memory, and to drive plotting devices that could put all the many levels of detail on paper. Today, much more sophisticated software is in use across the field, and CAD has become an industry norm.

REQUIREMENTS

High School

If you are interested in a career as a drafter, begin your preparation in high school. Load up on mathematics classes—especially algebra, geometry, and trigonometry. If your school offers courses in mechanical drawing, take as many as you can. If mechanical drawing is not available, take some art classes. Wood, metal, or electric shop may be helpful, depending on the field specialty in which you're interested. Geography or earth science courses are also useful. Finally, enroll in any computer classes you can; familiarity with technology will strengthen your job prospects.

Postsecondary Training

Preparation beyond high school (including courses in the physical sciences, mathematics, drawing, sketching and drafting techniques, and in other technical areas) is essential for certain types of beginning positions, as well as for advancement to positions of greater salary and more responsibility. This training is available through technical institutes, community colleges, and four-year colleges. The quality of programs varies greatly, however, and you should be careful about choosing one that meets your needs. Ask potential employers about their educational preferences, and check the qualifications of various schools' faculties. Generally, two-year community college programs that lead to an associate's degree offer a more well-rounded education than those provided by technical schools. Also, four-year colleges typically do not offer specific drafting training but have courses in areas such as engineering and architecture.

With respect to choosing a school for advanced training in drafting, exposure to CAD technology has become a necessity. Keep in mind, however, that CAD is a tool; it can help if manual drawing skill is not your strong suit. It does not replace knowledge and experience or creativity and imagination. A thorough grounding in the traditional drawing methods of drafting is as vitally important today as facility with CAD.

Certification or Licensing

Certification is not presently required but is recommended in this field. More and more, employers are looking for graduates whose skills have been approved by a reliable industry source. The American Design Drafting Association (ADDA) offers student certification services; taking advantage of them not only will enhance your credibility as a professional but could give you an edge in the job market. The test involved does not require specific knowledge of design or of computer programs, but is a general knowledge examination designed to help you demonstrate your level of expertise. It tests such areas of knowledge as geometric construction, working drawings, and architectural standards and terms.

ADDA also certifies schools that offer a drafting curriculum. As with individual certification, this accreditation process is not yet mandatory (although it can be a help to applicants in choosing where they'd like to receive training). Increasingly, however, states have begun to require that schools be ADDA-accredited (in order to receive grant funding, for instance). This suggests that required student certification, and perhaps licensing, may be on the horizon.

Other Requirements

Students interested in drafting should have a good sense of both spatial perception (the ability to visualize objects in two or three dimensions) and formal perception (the ability to compare and discriminate between shapes, lines, forms, and shadings). Good hand-eye coordination is also necessary for the fine-detail work involved in drafting.

EXPLORING

High school programs provide several opportunities for gaining experience in drafting. Mechanical drawing is a good course to take. There are also many hobbies and leisure activities, such as woodworking, building models, and repairing and remodeling projects, which require the preparation of drawings or use of blueprints. After the completion of some courses in mechanical drawing, it may be possible to locate a part-time or summer job in drafting.

EMPLOYERS

Approximately 254,000 drafters are employed in the United States. Drafters work in a wide range of disciplines, and companies that employ drafters may be found in many fields. A large percentage of drafters work in what might be considered the traditional positions—with architects or for engineering firms. Many work in manufacturing, however, in automotive or aerospace design, for heavy equipment manufacturers—almost anywhere where the end product must meet precise specifications. Other drafters work for construction, transportation, communications, or utilities companies or for local, state, or federal agencies. Approximately 44 percent of all drafters are employed by architectural, engineering, and related services firms. If a student has a particular interest in almost any field plus a desire to become a drafter, chances are good that he or she can find a job that will combine the two.

STARTING OUT

Beginning drafters generally have graduated from a postsecondary program at a technical institute or junior college. Skill certification through the American Design Drafting Association may be advantageous. Applicants for government positions may need to take a civil service examination. Beginning or inexperienced drafters often start as tracers. Students with some formal postsecondary technical training often qualify for positions as junior drafters who revise detail drawings and then gradually assume drawing assignments of a more complex nature.

ADVANCEMENT

With additional experience and skill, beginning drafters become checkers, detailers, design drafters, or senior drafters. Movement from one to another of these job classifications is not restricted; each business modifies work assignments based on its own needs. Drafters often move into related positions. Some typical positions include technical report writers, sales engineers, engineering assistants, production foremen, and installation technicians.

EARNINGS

Earnings in this field are dependent on a number of factors, including skills and experience. Students with more extensive advanced training tend to earn higher beginning salaries. Salaries also are affected by regional demands in specific specialties, so where a drafter chooses to live and work will play a part in his or her salary. According to the U.S. Department of Labor, median annual earnings of architectural and civil drafters were $40,390 in 2005, although earnings ranged from less than $26,140 for the lowest 10 percent to more than $59,590 for the highest 10 percent. Median annual earnings of mechanical drafters were $43,350 in 2005, with a range of less than $28,140 for the lowest 10 percent to over $67,410 for the highest 10 percent. Median earnings of electrical and electronics drafters were $45,550 a year in 2005. The lowest 10 percent of electrical and electronics drafters earned less than $29,040 a year, and the highest 10 percent earned more than $72,490. In general, full-time drafters earned from less than $25,230 to more than $74,120 a year.

Employers generally offer drafters a range of benefit options, including health insurance, retirement plans, and the like. Travel is sometimes considered an indirect benefit of a job. Although architects and engineers often travel to construction sites to inspect the development of individual projects, drafters seldom are required to travel. Construction drafters, for instance, may be asked to visit sites toward the end of construction to provide final drawings of the completed structure, but most of their work will be done from their offices.

WORK ENVIRONMENT

The drafter usually works in a well-lighted, air-conditioned, quiet room. This may be a central drafting room where drafters work side by side at large, tilted drawing tables or at computers. Some drafters work in an individual department, such as engineering, research, or development, where they work alone or with other drafters and with engineers, designers, or scientists. Occasionally, drafters may need to visit other departments or construction sites to consult with engineers or to gain firsthand information. In general, this is a desk job.

Most drafters work a 40-hour week with little overtime. Drafters work at drawing tables or computer stations for long periods of time, doing work that requires undivided concentration, close visual work, and very precise and accurate computations and drawings. There is generally little pressure, but occasionally last-minute design changes or a rush order may create tension or require overtime.

OUTLOOK

The U.S. Department of Labor predicts employment for drafters to increase more slowly than the average for all occupations through 2014. Increasing use of CAD technology will limit the demand for less-skilled drafters, but industrial growth and more complex designs of new products and manufacturing processes will increase the demand for drafting services. In addition, drafters are beginning to break out of the traditional drafting role and increasingly do work traditionally performed by engineers and architects. Nevertheless, job openings will be available as drafters leave the field for other positions or retirement. Opportunities will be best for well-educated drafters. Employment trends for drafters do fluctuate with the economy, however. During recessions, fewer buildings and manufactured products are designed, which could reduce the need for drafters in architectural, engineering, and manufacturing firms.

FOR MORE INFORMATION

For information on careers in drafting and certification, contact
American Design Drafting Association
105 East Main Street
Newbern, TN 38059-1526
Tel: 731-627-0802
Email: corporate@adda.org
http://www.adda.org

For news on laws affecting the field and other current topics, contact this union for the drafting community:
International Federation of Professional and Technical Engineers
8630 Fenton Street, Suite 400
Silver Spring, MD 20910-3828
Tel: 301-565-9016
http://www.ifpte.org

Electricians

QUICK FACTS

School Subjects
Mathematics
Technical/shop

Personal Skills
Mechanical/manipulative
Technical/scientific

Work Environment
Primarily indoors
Primarily multiple locations

Minimum Education Level
Apprenticeship

Salary Range
$25,870 to $42,790 to
$70,480+

Certification or Licensing
Required by certain states

Outlook
About as fast as the average

DOT
824

GOE
05.02.01, 05.02.02

NOC
2241

O*NET-SOC
47-2111.00

OVERVIEW

Electricians design, assemble, install, test, and repair electrical fixtures and wiring. They work on a wide range of electrical and data communications systems that provide light, heat, refrigeration, air conditioning, power, and the ability to communicate. There are approximately 656,000 electricians working in the United States.

HISTORY

It was during the latter part of the 19th century that electric power entered everyday life. Before then, electricity was the subject of experimentation and theorizing but had few practical applications. The widespread use of electricity was spurred by a combination of innovations—especially the discovery of a way to transmit power efficiently via overhead lines and the invention of the incandescent lamp, the telephone, and the electric telegraph. In the 1880s, commercial supplies of electricity began to be available in some cities, and within a few years, electric power was transforming many homes and factories.

Today, electricians are responsible for establishing and maintaining vital links between power-generating plants and the many electrical and electronic systems that shape our lives. Along with electricians who install and repair electrical systems for buildings, the field includes people who work on a wide array of telecommunications equipment, industrial machine-tool controls, marine facilities such as ships and offshore drilling rigs, and many other kinds of sophisticated equipment that have been developed using modern technology.

THE JOB

Many electricians specialize in either construction or maintenance work, although some work in both fields. Electricians in construction are usually employed by electrical contractors. Other *construction electricians* work for building contractors or industrial plants, public utilities, state highway commissions, or other large organizations that employ workers directly to build or remodel their properties. A few are self-employed.

When installing electrical systems, electricians may follow blueprints and specifications or may be told verbally what is needed. They may prepare sketches showing the intended location of wiring and equipment. Once the plan is clear, they measure, cut, assemble, and install plastic-covered wire or electrical conduit, which is a tube or channel through which heavier grades of electrical wire or cable are run. They strip insulation from wires, splice and solder wires together, and tape or cap the ends. They attach cables and wiring to the incoming electrical service and to various fixtures and machines that use electricity. They install switches, circuit breakers, relays, transformers, grounding leads, signal devices, and other electrical components. After the installation is complete, construction electricians test circuits for continuity and safety, adjusting the setup as needed.

Maintenance electricians do many of the same kinds of tasks, but their activities are usually aimed at preventing trouble before it occurs. They periodically inspect equipment and carry out routine service procedures, often according to a predetermined schedule. They repair or replace worn or defective parts and keep management informed about the reliability of the electrical systems. If any breakdowns occur, maintenance electricians return the equipment to full functioning as soon as possible so that the expense and inconvenience are minimal.

Maintenance electricians, also known as *electrical repairers,* may work in large factories, office buildings, small plants, or wherever existing electrical facilities and machinery need regular servicing to keep them in good working order. Many maintenance electricians work in manufacturing industries, such as those that produce automobiles, aircraft, ships, steel, chemicals, and industrial machinery. Some are employed by hospitals, municipalities, housing complexes, or shopping centers to do maintenance, repair, and sometimes installation work. Some work for or operate businesses that contract to repair and update wiring in residences and commercial buildings.

A growing number of electricians are involved in activities other than constructing and maintaining electrical systems in buildings.

An electrician repairs wiring in a fuse box. *(PhotoDisc)*

Many are employed to install computer wiring and equipment, telephone wiring, or the coaxial and fiber optic cables used in telecommunications and computer equipment. Electricians also work in power plants, where electric power is generated; in machine shops, where electric motors are repaired and rebuilt; aboard ships, fixing communications and navigation systems; at locations that need large lighting and power installations, such as airports and mines; and in numerous other settings.

All electricians must work in conformity with the National Electrical Code as well as any current state and local building and electrical codes. (Electrical codes are standards that electrical systems must meet to ensure safe, reliable functioning.) In doing their work, electricians try to use materials efficiently, to plan for future access to the area for service and maintenance on the system, and to avoid hazardous and unsightly wiring arrangements, making their work as neat and orderly as possible.

Electricians use a variety of equipment ranging from simple hand tools such as screwdrivers, pliers, wrenches, and hacksaws to power tools such as drills, hydraulic benders for metal conduit, and electric soldering guns. They also use testing devices such as oscilloscopes, ammeters, and test lamps. Construction electricians often supply their own hand tools. Experienced workers may have hundreds of dollars invested in tools.

REQUIREMENTS

High School
If you are thinking of becoming an electrician, whether you intend to enter an apprenticeship or learn informally on the job, you should

have a high school background that includes such courses as applied mathematics and science, shop classes that teach the use of various tools, and mechanical drawing. Electronics courses are especially important if you plan to become a maintenance electrician.

Postsecondary Training

Some electricians still learn their trade the same way electrical workers did many years ago—informally on the job while employed as helpers to skilled workers. Especially if that experience is supplemented with vocational or technical school courses, correspondence courses, or training received in the military, electrical helpers may in time become well-qualified crafts workers in some area of the field.

You should be aware, however, that most professionals believe that apprenticeship programs provide the best all-around training in this trade. Apprenticeships combine a series of planned, structured, supervised job experiences with classroom instruction in related subjects. Many programs are designed to give apprentices a variety of experiences by having them work for several electrical contractors doing different kinds of jobs. Typically, apprenticeships last four to five years and provide at least 144 hours of classroom instruction and 2,000 hours of on-the-job training each year. Completion of an apprenticeship is usually a significant advantage in getting the better jobs in the field.

Applicants for apprenticeships generally need to be high school graduates, at least 18 years of age, in good health, and with at least average physical strength. Although local requirements vary, many applicants are required to take tests to determine their aptitude for the work.

Most apprenticeship programs are developed and conducted by state and national contractor associations such as the Independent Electrical Contractors Inc. and the union locals of the International Brotherhood of Electrical Workers. Some programs are conducted as cooperative efforts between these groups and local community colleges and training organizations. In either situation, the apprenticeship program is usually managed by a training committee. An agreement regarding in-class and on-the-job training is usually established between the committee and each apprentice.

Certification or Licensing

Some states and municipalities require that electricians be licensed. To obtain a license, electricians usually must pass a written examination on electrical theory, National Electrical Code requirements, and local building and electrical codes. Electronics specialists receive certification training and testing through the International Society of Certified Electronic Technicians.

Other Requirements

You will need to have good color vision because electricians need to be able to distinguish color-coded wires. Agility and manual dexterity are also desirable characteristics, as are a sense of teamwork, an interest in working outdoors, and a love of working with your hands.

Electricians may or may not belong to a union. While many electricians belong to such organizations as the International Brotherhood of Electrical Workers; the International Union of Electronic, Electrical, Salaried, Machine, and Furniture Workers- Communications Workers of America; the International Association of Machinists and Aerospace Workers; and other unions, an increasing number of electricians are opting to affiliate with independent (nonunion) electrical contractors.

EXPLORING

Hobbies such as repairing radios, building electronics kits, or working with model electric trains will help you understand how electricians work. In addition to sampling related activities like these, you may benefit by arranging to talk with an electrician about his or her job. With the help of a teacher or guidance counselor, it may be possible to contact a local electrical contracting firm and locate someone willing to give an insider's description of the occupation.

EMPLOYERS

Approximately 656,000 electricians are employed in the United States. Electricians are employed in almost every industry imaginable, from construction to telecommunications to health care to transportation and more. Most work for contractors, but many work for institutional employers that require their own maintenance crews, or for government agencies. Some are self-employed.

STARTING OUT

People seeking to enter this field may either begin working as helpers or may enter an apprenticeship program. Leads for helper jobs may be located by contacting electrical contractors directly or by checking with the local offices of the state employment service or in newspaper classified advertising sections. Students in trade and vocational programs may be able to find job openings through the placement office of their school.

If you are interested in an apprenticeship, you may start by contacting the union local of the International Brotherhood of Electrical Workers, the local chapter of Independent Electrical Contractors Inc., or the local apprenticeship training committee. Information on apprenticeship possibilities also can be obtained through the state employment service.

ADVANCEMENT

Advancement possibilities for skilled, experienced electricians depend partly on their field of activity. Those who work in construction may become supervisors, job-site superintendents, or estimators for electrical contractors. Some electricians are able to establish their own contracting businesses, although in many areas contractors must obtain a special license. Another possibility for some electricians is to move, for example, from construction to maintenance work or into jobs in the shipbuilding, automobile, or aircraft industry.

Many electricians find that after they are working in the field, they still need to take courses to keep abreast of new developments. Unions and employers may sponsor classes introducing new methods and materials or explaining changes in electrical code requirements. By taking skill-improvement courses, electricians may also improve their chances for advancement to better-paying positions.

EARNINGS

Most established, full-time electricians working for contractors average earnings about $21 per hour, or $43,680 per year for full-time work, according to the National Joint Apprenticeship Training Committee— and it is possible to make much more. According to the U.S. Department of Labor, median hourly earnings of electricians were $20.57 in 2005 ($42,790 annually). Wages ranged from less than $12.44 for the lowest-paid 10 percent to more than $33.88 an hour for the highest-paid 10 percent, or from $25,870 to $70,480 yearly for full-time work. Beginning apprentices earn 40 percent of the base electrician's wage and receive periodic increases each year of their apprenticeship.

Overall, it's important to realize these wages can vary widely, depending on a number of factors, including geographic location, the industry in which an electrician works, prevailing economic conditions, union membership, and others. Wage rates for many electricians are set by contract agreements between unions and employers. In general, electricians working in cities tend to be better paid than those in other areas. Those working as telecommunications or residential specialists tend to make slightly less than those working as linemen or wiremen.

Electricians who are members of the International Brotherhood of Electrical Workers, the industry's labor union, are entitled to benefits including paid vacation days and holidays, health insurance, pensions to help with retirement savings, supplemental unemployment compensation plans, and so forth.

WORK ENVIRONMENT

Although electricians may work for the same contractor for many years, they work on different projects and at different work sites. In a single year, they may install wiring in a new housing project, rewire a factory, or install computer or telecommunications wiring in an office, for instance. Electricians usually work indoors, although some must do tasks outdoors or in buildings that are still under construction. The standard workweek is approximately 40 hours. In many jobs, overtime may be required. Maintenance electricians often have to work some weekend, holiday, or night hours because they must service equipment that operates all the time.

Electricians often spend long periods on their feet, sometimes on ladders or scaffolds or in awkward or uncomfortable places. The work can be strenuous. Electricians may have to put up with noise and dirt on the job. They may risk injuries such as falls from ladders, electrical shocks, and cuts and bruises. By following established safety practices, however, most of these hazards can be avoided.

OUTLOOK

Employment of electricians will grow about as fast as the average for all occupations through 2014, according to the U.S. Department of Labor. Growth will result from an overall increase in both residential and commercial construction. In addition, growth will be driven by the ever-expanding use of electrical and electronic devices and equipment. Electricians will be called on to upgrade old wiring and to install and maintain more extensive wiring systems than have been necessary in the past. In particular, the use of sophisticated computer, telecommunications, and data-processing equipment and automated manufacturing systems is expected to lead to job opportunities for electricians.

While the overall outlook for this occupational field is good, the availability of jobs will vary over time and from place to place. Construction activity fluctuates depending on the state of the local and national economy. Thus, during economic slowdowns, opportunities for construction electricians may not be plentiful. People working in this field need to be prepared for periods of unemployment between construction projects. Openings for apprentices also decline during economic downturns. Maintenance electricians are usually less vulnerable to periodic unemployment because they are more likely to work for one employer that needs electrical services on a steady basis. But if they work in an industry where the economy causes big fluctuations in the level of activity—such as automobile manufacturing, for instance—they may be laid off during recessions.

FOR MORE INFORMATION

For more information about the industry, contact
Independent Electrical Contractors
4401 Ford Avenue, Suite 1100
Alexandria, VA 22302-1432 Tel: 703-549-7351
Email: info@ieci.org
http://www.ieci.org

For information about the rules and benefits of joining a labor union, contact
International Brotherhood of Electrical Workers
900 Seventh Street, NW
Washington, DC 20001-3886
Tel: 202-833-7000
http://www.ibew.org and http://www.electrifyingcareers.com

For information on certification, contact
International Society of Certified Electronic Technicians
3608 Pershing Avenue
Fort Worth, TX 76107-4527
Tel: 800-946-0201
Email: info@iscet.org
http://www.iscet.org

For industry information, contact
National Electrical Contractors Association
3 Bethesda Metro Center, Suite 1100
Bethesda, MD 20814-6302
Tel: 301-657-3110
http://www.necanet.org

For background information on apprenticeship and training programs aimed at union workers, contact
National Joint Apprenticeship Training Committee
301 Prince George's Boulevard, Suite D
Upper Marlboro, MD 20774-7401
Email: office@njatc.org
http://www.njatc.org

Environmental Engineers

QUICK FACTS

School Subjects
Mathematics
Physics

Personal Skills
Leadership/management
Technical/scientific

Work Environment
Indoors and outdoors
Primarily multiple locations

Minimum Education Level
Bachelor's degree

Salary Range
$36,000 to $70,690 to
$104,610+

Certification or Licensing
Recommended

Outlook
Much faster than the average

DOT
005

GOE
02.03.03

NOC
2131

O*NET-SOC
17-2081.00

OVERVIEW

Environmental engineers design, build, and maintain systems to control waste streams produced by municipalities or private industry. Such waste streams may be wastewater, solid waste, hazardous waste, or contaminated emissions to the atmosphere (air pollution). Environmental engineers typically are employed by the Environmental Protection Agency (EPA), by private industry, or by engineering consulting firms. There are about 49,000 environmental engineers employed in the United States.

HISTORY

Although people have been doing work that falls into the category of environmental engineering for decades, only within about the last 30 years has a separate professional category has been recognized for environmental engineers.

Post-Civil War industrialization and urbanization created life-threatening water- and air-quality problems. These problems continued during and after World War II, dramatically increasing all forms of environmental pollution. After the war, pollution-control technologies were developed to deal with the damage.

"In the 1930s, 1940s, 1950s, even the 1960s, someone who wanted to be an environmental engineer would have been steered toward sanitary engineering, which basically deals with things like wastewater, putting sewers down," says Lee DeAngelis, regional director of the Environmental Careers Organization (ECO).

Sanitary engineering is a form of civil engineering. "Civil engineering is engineering for municipalities," explains Mike Waxman, who heads the environmental training arm of the outreach department at the University of Wisconsin-Madison College of Engineering. "It includes things like building roads, highways, buildings. But a big part of civil engineering is dealing with the waste streams that come from cities or municipalities. Wastewater from a city's sewage treatment plants is a prime example," Waxman says. This water must be treated in order to be pure enough to be used again. "Scientists work out what must be done to break down the harmful substances in the water, such as by adding bacteria; engineers design, build, and maintain the systems needed to carry this out. Technicians monitor the systems, take samples, run tests, and otherwise ensure that the system is working as it should."

This structure—scientists deciding what should be done at the molecular or biological level, engineers designing the systems needed to carry out the project, and technicians taking care of the day-to-day monitoring of the systems—is applied to other waste streams as well, Waxman adds.

Environmental engineering is an offshoot of civil engineering/sanitary engineering and focuses on the development of the physical systems needed to control waste streams. Civil engineers who already were doing this type of work began to refer to themselves as environmental engineers around 1970 with the great boom in new environmental regulations, according to Waxman. "It's what they wanted to be called," he says. "They wanted the recognition for what they were doing."

THE JOB

There is a small pond in Crawford County, Illinois, that provides the habitat and primary food source for several different species of fish, frogs, turtles, insects, and birds, as well as small mammals. About a half-mile away is the Jack J. Ryan and Sons Manufacturing Company. For years, this plant has safely treated its wastewater—produced during the manufacturing process—and discharged it into the pond. Then one day, without warning, hundreds of dead fish wash up on the banks of the pond. What's going on? What should be done? It is the job of environmental engineers to investigate and design a system to make the water safe for the flora and fauna that depend on it for survival.

Environmental engineers who work for the federal or state Environmental Protection Agency (EPA) act as police officers or detectives. They investigate problems stemming from systems that aren't functioning properly. They have knowledge about wastewater treatment systems and have the authority to enforce environmental regulations.

The Crawford County pond is in the jurisdiction of the Champaign regional office of the Illinois Environmental Protection Agency

(IEPA). There are three divisions: air, land, and water. An environmental engineer in the water division is alerted to the fish kill at the pond and head out to the site to investigate. The engineer takes photographs and samples of the water and makes notes to document the problem. He or she considers the possibilities: Is it a discharge problem from Jack J. Ryan and Sons? If so, was there an upset in the process? A spill? A flood? Could a storage tank be leaking? Or is the problem upstream? The pond is connected to other waterways, so could some other discharger be responsible for killing the fish?

The engineer visits Jack J. Ryan and Sons to talk to the production manager and ask if the plant has been doing anything differently lately. The investigation might include a tour of the plant or an examination of its plans. It might also include questioning other manufacturers farther upstream to see if they are doing something new that's caused the fish kill.

Once the problem has been identified, the environmental engineer and the plant officials can work together on the solution. For example, the production manager at Jack J. Ryan and Sons reports that they've changed something in the manufacturing process to produce a new kind of die-cast part. They didn't know they were doing something wrong. The EPA engineer informs the company they'll be fined $10,000, and a follow-up investigation will be conducted to make sure it has complied with regulations.

Jack J. Ryan and Sons may have its own environmental engineer on staff. This engineer's job is to help keep the company in compliance with federal and state regulations while balancing the economic concerns of the company. At one time, industries' environmental affairs positions were often filled by employees who also had other positions in the plant. Since the late 1980s, however, these positions have been held by environmental experts, including scientists, engineers, lawyers, and communications professionals.

In the Crawford County pond scenario, a Ryan and Sons environmental expert might get a call from an engineer at the IEPA: "There seems to be a fish kill at the pond near your plant. We've determined it's probably from a discharge from your plant." The Ryan and Sons expert looks at the plant's plans, talks to the production manager, and figures out a plan of action to bring the company into compliance.

Some companies rely on environmental engineering consulting firms instead of keeping an engineer on staff. Consulting firms usually provide teams that visit the plant, assess the problem, and design a system to get the plant back into compliance. Consulting firms not only know the technical aspects of waste control but also have expertise in dealing with the government—filling out the required government forms, for example.

Broadly speaking, environmental engineers may focus on one of three areas: air, land, or water. Those concerned with air work on air-pollution control, air-quality management, and other specialties involved in systems to treat emissions. The private sector tends to have the majority of these jobs, according to the Environmental Careers Organization. Environmental engineers focused on land include landfill professionals, for whom environmental engineering and public health are key areas. Engineers focused on water work on activities similar to those described above.

A big area for environmental engineers is hazardous waste management. Expertise in designing systems and processes to reduce, recycle, and treat hazardous waste streams is very much in demand, according to ECO. This area tends to be the most technical of all the environmental fields and thus demands more professionals with graduate and technical degrees.

Environmental engineers spend a lot of time on paperwork—including writing reports and memos and filling out forms. They also might climb a smokestack, wade in a creek, or go toe-to-toe with a district attorney in a battle over a compliance matter. If they work on company staffs, they may face frustration over not knowing what is going on in their own plants. If they work for the government, they might struggle with bureaucracy. If they work for a consultant, they may have to juggle the needs of the client (including the need to keep costs down) with the demands of the government.

REQUIREMENTS

High School
A bachelor's degree is mandatory to work in environmental engineering. At the high school level, the most important course work is in science and mathematics. It's also good to develop written communication skills. Competition to get into the top engineering schools is tough, so it's important to do well on your ACT or SAT tests.

Postsecondary Training
About 20 schools offer an undergraduate degree in environmental engineering. Another possibility is to earn a civil engineering, mechanical engineering, industrial engineering, or other traditional engineering degree with an environmental focus. You could also obtain a traditional engineering degree and learn environmental knowledge on the job or obtain a master's degree in environmental engineering.

Certification or Licensing
If your work as an engineer affects public health, safety, or property, you must register with the state. To obtain registration, you must

have a degree from an accredited engineering program. Right before you get your degree (or soon after), you must pass an engineer-in-training (EIT) exam covering fundamentals of science and engineering. A few years after you've started your career, you also must pass an exam covering engineering practice. Additional certification is voluntary and may be obtained through such organizations as the American Academy of Environmental Engineers.

Other Requirements
Environmental engineers must like solving problems and have a good background in science and math. They must be able to, in the words of one engineer, "just get in there and figure out what needs to be done." Engineers must be able to communicate verbally and in writing with a variety of people from both technical and nontechnical backgrounds.

EXPLORING

A good way to explore becoming an environmental engineer is to talk to someone in the field. Contact your local EPA office, check the Yellow Pages for environmental consulting firms in your area, or ask a local industrial company if you can visit. The latter is not as far-fetched as you might think; Big industry has learned the value of earning positive community relations, and their outreach efforts may include having an open house for their neighbors in which one can walk through their plants, ask questions, and get a feel for what goes on there.

You cannot practice being an environmental engineer without having a bachelor's degree. However, you can put yourself in situations in which you're around environmental engineers to see what they do and how they work. To do so, you may volunteer for the local chapter of a nonprofit environmental organization, do an internship through ECO or another organization, or work first as an environmental technician, a job that requires less education (such as a two-year associate's degree or even a high school diploma).

Another good way to get exposure to environmental engineering is to familiarize yourself with professional journals. Two journals that may be available in your library include *Chemical & Engineering News,* which regularly features articles on waste management systems, and *Pollution Engineering,* which features articles of interest to environmental engineers.

EMPLOYERS

Approximately 49,000 environmental engineers are employed in the United States. Environmental engineers most often work for the

Environmental Protection Agency (EPA), in private industry, or at engineering consulting firms.

STARTING OUT

The traditional method of entering this field is by obtaining a bachelor's degree and applying directly to companies or to the EPA. School career services offices can assist you in these efforts.

ADVANCEMENT

After environmental engineers have gained work experience, there are several routes for advancement. Those working for the EPA can become a department supervisor or switch to private industry or consulting. In-house environmental staff members may rise to supervisory positions. Engineers with consulting firms may become project managers or specialists in certain areas.

Environmental careers are evolving at breakneck speed. New specialties are emerging all the time. Advancement may take the form of getting involved at the beginning stages of a new subspecialty that suits an engineer's particular interests, experience, and expertise.

EARNINGS

The U.S. Department of Labor reports that mean annual earnings of environmental engineers employed in architectural and engineering services were $70,690 in 2005. Salaries for environmental engineers employed in all fields ranged from less than $42,570 for the lowest-paid 10 percent to more than $104,610 for the highest-paid 10 percent. According to a 2005 salary survey by the National Association of Colleges and Employers, bachelor's degree candidates in environmental/environmental health received starting offers averaging $ 47,384 a year.

According to the American Academy of Environmental Engineers, engineers with a bachelor of science degree were receiving starting salaries ranging from $36,000 to $42,000 with some as much as $48,000 in the late 1990s. Those with a master's degree earned $40,000 to $45,000, and those with a Ph.D. earned $42,000 to $50,000. Licensed engineers with five years of experience can expect to earn from $50,000 to $60,000.

Fringe benefits vary widely depending on the employer. State EPA jobs may include, for example, two weeks of vacation, health insurance, tuition reimbursement, use of company vehicles for work, and similar perks. In-house or consulting positions may add additional benefits to lure top candidates.

> ## Learn More About It
>
> Bellandi, Robert. (ed.) *Strategic Environmental Management for Engineers.* Hoboken, N.J.: Wiley, 2004.
> Berthouex, Paul Mac, and Linfield C. Brown. *Statistics for Environmental Engineers.* 2nd ed. Boca Raton, Fla.: CRC Press, 2002.
> McGraw-Hill. *Dictionary of Engineering.* 2nd ed. New York: McGraw-Hill Professional, 2003.
> Salvato, Joseph A., Nelson L. Nemerow, and Franklin J. Agardy. *Environmental Engineering.* 5th ed. Hoboken, N.J.: Wiley, 2003.
> Spellman, Frank R. *Environmental Engineer's Mathematics Handbook.* Boca Raton, Fla.: CRC Press, 2004.
> Thomas, Randall. *Environmental Design: An Introduction for Architects and Engineers.* New York: Spon Press, 1999.

WORK ENVIRONMENT

Environmental engineers split their time between working in an office and working in the field. They may also spend time in courtrooms. Since ongoing education is crucial in most of these positions, engineers must attend training sessions and workshops and study new regulations, techniques, and problems. They usually work as part of a team that may include any of a number of different specialists. Engineers must also give presentations of technical information to those with both technical and nontechnical backgrounds.

OUTLOOK

The *Occupational Outlook Handbook* projects that employment for environmental engineers will grow much faster than the average for all occupations through 2014. Engineers will be needed to clean up existing hazards and help companies comply with government regulations. The shift toward prevention of problems and protecting public health should create job opportunities.

Jobs are available with all three major employers—the EPA, industry, and consulting firms. The EPA has long been a big employer of environmental engineers.

FOR MORE INFORMATION

For information on certification, careers, and salaries or a copy of Environmental Engineering Selection Guide *(giving names of accredited environmental engineering programs and of professors who have board certification as environmental engineers), contact*

American Academy of Environmental Engineers
130 Holiday Court, Suite 100
Annapolis, MD 21401-7003
Tel: 410-266-3311
http://www.aaee.net

For information on internships and career guidance, contact
Environmental Careers Organization
30 Winter Street
Boston, MA 02108-4720
Tel: 617-426-4783
http://www.eco.org

For career guidance information contact
Junior Engineering Technical Society Inc.
1420 King Street, Suite 405
Alexandria, VA 22314-2794
Tel: 703-548-5387
Email: info@jets.orghttp://www.jets.org

The following is a cross-disciplinary environmental association:
National Association of Environmental Professionals
PO Box 2086
Bowie, MD 20718-2086
Tel: 888-251-9902
Email: office@naep.org
http://www.naep.org

For information about the private waste services industry, contact
National Solid Wastes Management Association
4301 Connecticut Avenue, NW, Suite 300
Washington, DC 20008-2304
Tel: 202-244-4700
http://www.nswma.org

Contact SCA for information about internships for high school students.
Student Conservation Association (SCA)
689 River Road
PO Box 550
Charlestown, NH 03603-0550
Tel: 603-543-1700
http://www.sca-inc.org

Heating and Cooling Technicians

QUICK FACTS

School Subjects
Mathematics
Technical/shop

Personal Skills
Following instructions
Mechanical/manipulative

Work Environment
Indoors and outdoors
Primarily multiple locations

Minimum Education Level
High school diploma
Apprenticeship

Salary Range
$22,970 to $37,040 to
$57,130+

Certification or Licensing
Required for certain
positions

Outlook
Faster than the average

DOT
637

GOE
05.03.01

NOC
7313

O*NET-SOC
49-9021.00, 49-9021.01,
49-9021.02

OVERVIEW

Heating and cooling technicians work on systems that control the temperature, humidity, and air quality of enclosed environments. They help design, manufacture, install, and maintain climate-control equipment. They provide people with heating and air conditioning in such structures as shops, hospitals, malls, theaters, factories, restaurants, offices, apartment buildings, and private homes. They may work to provide temperature-sensitive products such as computers, foods, medicines, and precision instruments with climate-controlled environments. They may also provide comfortable environments or refrigeration in such modes of transportation as ships, trucks, planes, and trains. There are approximately 270,000 heating and cooling technicians employed in the United States.

HISTORY

The modern heating industry got its start with the appearance of piped steam heating during the Industrial Revolution. Piped hot water heating replaced steam in the 1830s because of its improved comfort level and lower temperature requirement. Oil and coal heat in the late 19th and early 20th centuries have largely been superceded by today's natural gas and electric heating. Heading into the 21st century, radiant heat and geothermal heating are becoming more important within the heating industry.

Cooling or air-conditioning mechanisms were virtually unknown until 1842, when Dr. John Gorrie invented a cold-air machine to relieve the suffering of yellow fever patients in a Florida hospital. Naturally occurring ice was relied upon for refrigeration until shortly after the Civil War, when a process to produce artificial ice was invented and put to use in the southern states. The development of synthetic refrigerant gases in the early 20th century led to the widespread use of mechanical refrigeration by the 1930s and home air conditioning by the 1950s.

Initially, the equipment for limited-capacity air conditioning, refrigeration, and heating systems was simple, and the skills needed to maintain them were comparatively easy to learn. Most technicians for this early equipment were trained by manufacturers and distributors. But as the field has expanded and the equipment has become much more sophisticated, workers have had to pursue more specialized knowledge and skills.

THE JOB

Many industries today depend on carefully controlled temperature and humidity conditions while manufacturing, transporting, or storing their products. Many common foods are readily available only because of extensive refrigeration. Less obviously, numerous chemicals, drugs, explosives, oil, and other products our society uses must be produced using refrigeration processes. For example, some room-sized computer systems need to be kept at a certain temperature and humidity; spacecraft must be able to withstand great heat while exposed to the rays of the sun and great cold when the moon or earth blocks the sun and at the same time maintain a steady internal environment; the air in tractor-trailer cabs must be regulated so that truck drivers can spend long hours behind the wheel in maximum comfort and safety. Each of these applications represents a different segment of a large and very diverse industry.

Heating and cooling technicians may work in installation and maintenance (which includes service and repairs), sales, or manufacturing. The majority of technicians who work in installation and maintenance work for heating and cooling contractors; manufacturers of air-conditioning, refrigeration, and heating equipment; dealers and distributors; or utility companies.

Technicians who assemble and install air-conditioning, refrigeration, and heating systems and equipment work from blueprints. Experienced technicians read blueprints that show them how to assemble components and how the components should be installed into the structure. Because structure sizes and climate-control specifications vary, technicians have to pay close attention to blueprint details. While working from the blueprints, technicians use algebra and geometry to calculate the sizes and contours of duct work as they assemble it.

Heating and cooling technicians work with a variety of hardware, tools, and components. For example, in joining pipes and duct work for an air-conditioning system, technicians may use soldering, welding, or brazing equipment, as well as sleeves, couplings, and elbow joints. Technicians handle and assemble such components as motors, thermometers, burners, compressors, pumps, and fans. They must join these parts together when building climate-control units and then connect this equipment to the duct work, refrigerant lines, and power source.

As a final step in assembly and installation, technicians run tests on equipment to ensure that it functions properly. If the equipment is malfunctioning, technicians must investigate in order to diagnose the problem and determine a solution. At this time, they adjust thermostats, reseal piping, and replace parts as needed. They retest the equipment to determine whether the problem has been remedied, and they continue to modify and test it until everything checks out as functioning properly.

Some technicians may specialize on only one type of cooling, heating, or refrigeration equipment. For example, *window air-conditioning unit installers and servicers* work on window units only. *Air-conditioning and refrigeration technicians* install and service central air-conditioning systems and a variety of refrigeration equipment. Air-conditioning installations may range from small wall units, either water- or air-cooled, to large central plant systems. Commercial refrigeration equipment may include display cases, walk-in coolers, and frozen-food units such as those in supermarkets, restaurants, and food-processing plants.

Other technicians are *furnace installers,* also called *heating-equipment installers.* Following blueprints and other specifications, they install oil, gas, electric, solid fuel (such as coal), and multifuel heating systems. They move the new furnace into place and attach fuel supply lines, air ducts, pumps, and other components. Then they connect the electrical wiring and thermostatic controls and, finally, check the unit for proper operation.

Technicians who work in maintenance perform routine service to keep systems operating efficiently and respond to service calls for repairs. They perform tests and diagnose problems on equipment that has been installed in the past. They calibrate controls, add fluids, change parts, clean components, and test the system for proper operation. For example, in performing a routine service call on a furnace, technicians will adjust blowers and burners, replace filters, clean ducts, and check thermometers and other controls.

Technicians who maintain oil- and gas-burning equipment are called *oil-burner mechanics* and *gas-burner mechanics,* or *gas-appliance servicers.* They usually perform more extensive maintenance work during warm weather, when the heating system can be shut down. During the summer, technicians replace oil and air filters; vacuum vents, ducts, and other parts that accumulate soot and ash; and adjust the burner so that it achieves maximum operating efficiency. Gas-burner mechanics may also repair other gas appliances such as cooking stoves, clothes dryers, water heaters, outdoor lights, and grills.

Other heating and cooling technicians who specialize in a limited range of equipment include evaporative cooler installers; hot-air furnace installer-and-repairers; solar-energy system installers and helpers; and air and hydronic balancing technicians, radiant heating installers, and geothermal heating and cooling technicians. In their work on refrigerant lines and air ducts, heating and cooling technicians use a variety of hand and power tools, including hammers, wrenches, metal snips, electric drills, measurement gauges, pipe cutters and benders, and acetylene torches. To check electrical circuits, burners, and other components, technicians work with volt-ohmmeters, manometers, and other testing devices.

REQUIREMENTS

High School

In high school, students considering the heating and cooling field should take algebra, geometry, English composition, physics, computer applications and programming, and classes in industrial arts or shop. Helpful shop classes include mechanical drawing and blueprint reading, power and hand tools operations, and metalwork. Shop courses in electricity and electronics provide a strong introduction into understanding circuitry and wiring and teach students to read electrical diagrams. Classes in computer-aided design are also helpful, as are business courses.

Postsecondary Training

Although postsecondary training is not mandatory to become a heating, air-conditioning, and refrigeration technician, employers prefer to hire technicians who have training from a technical school, junior college, or apprenticeship program. Vocational-technical schools, private trade schools, and junior colleges offer both one- and two-year programs. Graduates of two-year programs usually receive an associate's degree in science or in applied science. Certificates, rather than degrees, are awarded to those who complete one-year programs. Although no formal education is required, most employers prefer to hire graduates of two-year applications-oriented training programs. This kind of training includes a strong background in mathematical and engineering theory. However, the emphasis is on the practical uses of such theories, not on explorations of their origins and development, such as one finds in engineering programs. The following organizations accredit heating and cooling technology programs: HVAC Excellence, the National Center for Construction Education and Research, and the Partnership for Air-Conditioning, Heating, and Refrigeration Accreditation.

Formal apprenticeship programs typically last three to five years and combine classroom education with on-the-job training. Programs are offered by local chapters of the following organizations: Air Conditioning Contractors of America; Mechanical Contractors Association of America; Plumbing-Heating-Cooling Contractors Association; Sheet Metal Workers International Association; United Association of Journeymen and Apprentices of the Plumbing and Pipefitting Industry of the United States and Canada; Associated Builders and Contractors; and National Association of Home Builders.

Certification or Licensing

Voluntary certification for various specialties is available through professional associations. The heating and cooling industry recently adopted a standard certification program for experienced technicians. The program is available to both installation and service technicians and is offered by North American Technician Excellence Inc. Technicians must take and pass a core exam (covering safety, tools, soft skills, principles of heat transfer, and electrical systems) and one specialty exam of their choice (covering installation and service). The specialties available are air conditioning, air distribution, gas heating, heat pumps, hydronics, and oil heating. Technicians who become certified as service technicians are automatically certified as installation technicians without additional testing. Certification must be renewed every five years.

The Refrigerating Engineers and Technicians Association offers the certified assistant refrigeration operator and certified industrial refrigeration operator designations to heating and cooling technicians who specialize in industrial-plant refrigeration. Contact the association for more information. The Air-Conditioning and Refrigeration Institute offers certification to technicians who work for the Environmental Protection Agency. HVAC Excellence offers certification to professionals at a variety of skill levels.

Technicians who handle refrigerants must receive approved refrigerant recovery certification, which is a requirement of the Environmental Protection Agency (EPA) and requires passing a special examination. The following certifications levels are available: Type I (servicing small appliances), Type II (high-pressure refrigerants), and Type III (low-pressure refrigerants). Exams are administered by unions, trade schools, and contractor associations approved by the EPA.

In some areas of the field (for example, those who work with design and research engineers), certification is increasingly the norm and viewed as a basic indicator of competence. Even where there are no firm requirements, it generally is better to be qualified for whatever license or certification is available.

Other Requirements

Persons interested in the heating and cooling field need to have an aptitude for working with tools, manual dexterity and manipulation, and the desire to perform challenging work that requires a high level of competence and quality. Students interested in how things work, who enjoy taking things apart and putting them back together, and who enjoy troubleshooting for mechanical and electrical problems may enjoy a career in air-conditioning, refrigeration, and heating.

EXPLORING

A student trying to decide on a career in heating and cooling technology may have to base the choice on a variety of indirect evidence. Part-time or summer work is usually not available to high school students, because of their lack of the necessary skills and knowledge. It may be possible, however, to arrange field trips to service shops, companies that develop and produce heating and cooling equipment, or other firms concerned with the environmental-control field. Such visits can provide a firsthand overview of the day-to-day work. A visit with a local contractor or to a school that conducts a heating and cooling technology training program can also be very helpful.

EMPLOYERS

Approximately 270,000 heating and cooling technicians are employed in the United States. While most heating and cooling technicians work directly with the building, installation, and maintenance of equipment via heating and cooling firms, some technicians work in equipment sales. These technicians are usually employed by manufacturers or dealers and distributors and are hired to explain the equipment and its operation to prospective customers. These technicians must have a thorough knowledge of their products. They may explain newly developed equipment, ideas, and principles, or assist dealers and distributors in the layout and installation of unfamiliar components. Some technicians employed as sales representatives contact prospective buyers and help them plan air-conditioning, refrigeration, and heating systems. They help the client select appropriate equipment and estimate costs.

Other technicians work for manufacturers in engineering or research laboratories, performing many of the same assembling and testing duties as technicians who work for contractors. However, they perform these operations at the manufacturing site rather than traveling to work sites as most contractors' technicians do. Technicians aid engineers in research, equipment design, and equipment testing. Technicians in a research laboratory may plan the requirements for the various stages of fabricating, installing, and servicing climate-control and refrigeration systems; recommend appropriate equipment to meet specified needs; and calculate heating and cooling capacities of proposed equipment units. They also may conduct operational tests on experimental models and efficiency tests on new units coming off the production lines. They might also investigate the cause of breakdowns reported by customers and determine the reasons and solutions.

Engineering-oriented technicians employed by manufacturers may perform tests of new equipment or assist engineers in fundamental research and development, technical report writing, and application engineering. Other engineering technicians serve as *liaison representatives*, coordinating the design and production engineering for the development and manufacture of new products.

Technicians may also be employed by utility companies to help ensure that their customers' equipment is using energy efficiently and effectively. *Utility technicians*, often called *energy conservation technicians*, may conduct energy evaluations of customers' systems, compile energy surveys, and provide customer information.

Technicians may also work for consulting firms, such as engineering firms or building contractors who hire technicians to estimate costs, determine air-conditioning and heating load requirements, and prepare specifications for climate-control projects.

Heating and cooling technicians must have an aptitude for working with tools. *(Jim Whitmer Photograpy)*

Some large institutions such as hospitals, universities, factories, office complexes, and sports arenas employ heating and cooling technicians directly, maintaining their own climate-control staffs.

Some technicians also open up their own businesses, either as heating and cooling contractors or consultants specializing in sales, parts supply, service, and installation.

STARTING OUT

Many students in two-year programs work at a job related to their area of training during the summer between the first and second years. Their employers may hire them on a part-time basis during the second year and make offers of full-time employment after graduation. Even if such a job offer cannot be made, the employer may be aware of other companies that are hiring and help the student with suggestions and recommendations, provided the student's work record is good.

Some schools make work experience part of the curriculum, particularly during the latter part of their program. This is a valuable way for students to gain practical experience in conjunction with classroom work.

It is not unusual for graduates of two-year programs to receive several offers of employment, either from contacts they have made themselves or from companies that routinely recruit new graduates. Representatives of larger companies often schedule interview periods at schools with two-year air-conditioning, refrigeration, and heating technician programs. Other, usually smaller, prospective employers may contact specific faculty advisors who in turn make students aware of opportunities that arise.

In addition to using their schools' job placement services, resourceful students can independently explore other leads by applying directly to local heating and cooling contractors; sales, installation, and service shops; or manufacturers of air-conditioning, refrigeration, and heating equipment. State employment offices may also post openings or provide job leads. Finally, student membership in the local chapter of a trade association, such as one of those listed at the end of this article, will often result in good employment contacts.

ADVANCEMENT

There is such a wide range of positions within this field that workers who gain the necessary skills and experience have the flexibility to choose among many different options and types of positions. As employees gain on-the-job work experience, they may decide to specialize in a particular aspect or type of work. They may be able to be promoted into positions requiring more responsibilities and skills through experience and demonstrated proficiency, but in some cases additional training is required.

Many workers continue to take courses throughout their careers to upgrade their skills and to learn new techniques and methods used within the industry. Training can take the form of a class offered by a manufacturer regarding specific equipment or may be a more extensive program resulting in certification for a specific area or procedure. Skill-improvement programs that offer advanced training in specialized areas are available through vocational-technical institutes and trade associations. Technicians with an interest in the engineering aspect of the industry may go back to school to get a bachelor of science degree in heating and cooling engineering or mechanical engineering.

Technicians increase their value to employers and themselves with continued training. For example, a technician employed by a manufacturer may progress to the position of *sales manager,* who acts as liaison with distributors and dealers, promoting and selling the manufacturer's products, or to a *field service representative,* who solves unusual service problems of dealers and distributors in the area. Technicians working for dealers and distributors or contractors may advance to a *service manager* or supervisory position, overseeing other technicians who install and service equipment. Another possible specialization is mechanical design, which involves designing piping, duct work, controls, and the distribution systems for consulting engineers, mechanical contractors, manufacturers, and distributors. Technicians who do installation and maintenance may decide to move into sales or work for the research and development department of a manufacturing company.

Some technicians also open up their own businesses, becoming heating and cooling contractors, consultants, self-employed service technicians, or specializing in sales and parts distribution.

EARNINGS

The earnings of heating and cooling technicians vary widely according to the level of training and experience, the nature of their work, type of employer, region of the country, and other factors. Heating and cooling technicians had median hourly earnings of $17.81 (or $37,040 annually) in 2005, according to the U.S. Department of Labor. The lowest 10 percent earned less than $11.04 (or $22,970 annually), while the top 10 percent earned more than $27.46 (or $57,130 annually).

Heating and cooling apprentices usually earn about 50 percent of the wage rate paid to experienced workers. This percentage rises as apprentices gain experience and skill training in the field.

Many employers offer medical insurance and paid vacation days, holidays, and sick days, although the actual benefits vary from employer to employer. Some companies also offer tuition assistance for additional training.

WORK ENVIRONMENT

Working conditions for heating and cooling technicians vary considerably, depending on the area of the industry in which they work. For the most part, the hours are regular, although certain jobs in production may involve shift work, and service technicians may have to be on call some evenings and weekends to handle emergency repairs.

Technicians who work in installation and service may work in a variety of environments ranging from industrial plants to construction sites and can include both indoor and outdoor work. Technicians may encounter extremes in temperature when servicing outdoor and rooftop equipment and cramped quarters when servicing indoor commercial and industrial equipment. They often have to lift heavy objects as well as stoop, crawl, and crouch when making repairs and installations. Working conditions can include dirt, grease, noise, and safety hazards. Hazards include falls from rooftops or scaffolds, electric shocks, burns, and handling refrigerants and compressed gases. With proper precautions and safety measures, however, the risk from these hazards can be minimized.

Technicians who work in laboratories usually work in the research and development departments of a manufacturing firm or an industrial plant. Technicians employed by distributors, dealers, and consulting engineers usually work in an office or similar surroundings and are subject to the same benefits and conditions as other office workers. Some technicians, such as sales representatives or service managers, go out periodically to visit customers or installation and service sites.

OUTLOOK

Employment in the heating and cooling field is expected to increase faster than the average for all occupations through 2014, according to the U.S. Department of Labor. Some openings will occur when experienced workers retire or transfer to other work. Other openings will be generated because of a demand for new climate-control systems for residences and industrial and commercial users. In addition, many existing systems are being upgraded to provide more efficient use of energy and to provide benefits not originally built into the system. There is a growing emphasis on improving indoor air and making equipment more environmentally friendly. Systems that use chloroflurocarbons (CFCs) need to be retrofitted or replaced with new equipment, since regulations banning CFC production became effective in 2000.

Comfort is only one of the major reasons for environmental control. Conditioned atmosphere is a necessity in any precision industry where temperature and humidity can affect fine tolerances. As products and processes become more complex and more highly automated, the need for closely controlled conditions becomes increasingly important. For example, electronics manufacturers must keep the air bone-dry for many parts of their production processes to prevent damage to parts and to maintain nonconductivity. Pharmaceutical and food manufacturers rely on pure, dirt-free air. High-speed multicolor printing requires temperature control of rollers and moisture control for the paper racing through the presses. There is every reason to expect that these and other sophisticated industries will rely more in the coming years on precision control of room conditions. The actual amount of industry growth for these applications will hinge on the overall health of the nation's economy and the rate of manufacturing.

Technicians involved in maintenance and repair are not as affected by the economy as workers in some other jobs. Whereas in bad economic times a consumer may postpone building a new house or installing a new air-conditioning system, hospitals, restaurants, technical industries, and public buildings will still require skilled technicians to maintain their climate-control systems. Technicians versed in more than one aspect of the job have greater job flexibility and can count on fairly steady work despite any fluctuations in the economy.

FOR MORE INFORMATION

For information on certification and publications, contact
Air-Conditioning and Refrigeration Institute
4100 North Fairfax Drive, Suite 200
Arlington, VA 22203-1623
Tel: 703-524-8800
Email: ari@ari.org
http://www.ari.org

For information on careers and educational programs, contact
Air Conditioning Contractors of America
2800 Shirlington Road, Suite 300
Arlington, VA 22206-3607
Tel: 703-575-4477
Email: info@acca.org
http://www.acca.org

For information on careers, contact
American Society of Heating, Refrigerating and Air-Conditioning Engineers Inc.
1791 Tullie Circle, NE
Atlanta, GA 30329-2305
Tel: 404-636-8400

Email: ashrae@ashrae.org
http://www.ashrae.org

For information on accredited programs and certification, contact
HVAC Excellence
PO Box 491
Mt. Prospect, IL 60056-0491
Tel: 800-394-5268
http://www.hvacexcellence.org

For information on certification programs, contact
North American Technician Excellence Inc.
4100 North Fairfax Drive, Suite 210
Arlington, VA 22203-1623
Tel: 877-420-NATE
http://www.natex.org

For information on accredited training programs, contact
**Partnership for Air-Conditioning, Heating, Refrigeration
  Accreditation**
4100 North Fairfax Drive, Suite 210
Arlington, VA 22203-1623
Email: pahra@pahrahvacr.org
http://www.pahrahvacr.org

For information on union membership, contact
Plumbing-Heating-Cooling Contractors Association
PO Box 6808
180 South Washington Street
Falls Church, VA 22046-2900
Tel: 800-533-7694
Email: naphcc@naphcc.org
http://www.phccweb.org

*For information on industrial plant refrigeration certification,
contact*
Refrigerating Engineers & Technicians Association
PO Box 1819
Salinas, CA 93902-1819
Tel: 831-455-8783
Email: info@reta.com
http://www.reta.com

For information on heating and cooling and the sheet metal indus-try, contact

Sheet Metal and Air Conditioning Contractors' National Association
4201 Lafayette Center Drive
Chantilly, VA 20151-1209
Tel: 703-803-2980
Email: info@smacna.org
http://www.smacna.org

Check out the following Web site, created by a coalition of organi-zations representing the heating, air-conditioning, and refrigeration industry:

Cool Careers
Email: info@coolcareers.org
http://www.coolcareers.org

Historic Preservationists

QUICK FACTS

School Subjects
Art
History

Personal Skills
Artistic
Helping/teaching

Work Environment
Indoors and outdoors
Primarily multiple locations

Minimum Education Level
Bachelor's degree

Salary Range
$24,340 to $44,400 to
$83,960+

Certification or Licensing
None available

Outlook
About as fast as the average

DOT
052

GOE
11.03.03

NOC
4169

O*NET-SOC
19-3093.00

OVERVIEW

Historic preservationists are champions of buildings and sites of historic or cultural significance. Their duties include the identification, evaluation, protection, and renovation of parks, structures, buildings, or entire neighborhoods. They may also help manage ongoing maintenance of restored structures or sites.

HISTORY

Many historians agree the first major restoration project documented in the United States was Mount Vernon, the home of George Washington, the first president of the United States. In 1889, a group of women concerned about the state of President Washington's home formed the Mount Vernon's Ladies Association and restored the mansion and grounds to its former glory.

Also in 1889, the Association of the Preservation of Virginia's Antiquities became the first statewide historic group in the United States. The organization, now known as APVA Preservation Virginia, owns and maintains various historically important sites throughout the state of Virginia.

The biggest boost to the preservation movement was the passage of the 1966 National Historic Preservation Act. The law reinforced the government's commitment to caring for the nation's historic treasures. From then on, defining, restoring, and maintaining sites and structures were done according to a certain standard.

The National Park Service (NPS) is a federal bureau of the U.S. Department of the Interior responsible for resources owned by the government, such as archeological sites, battlefields, natural landscapes, monuments, and historical homes. The NPS also sets regulations under which privately owned historical districts are managed. The NPS administers many agencies devoted to cultural and historical resources. One agency, the National Register of Historic Places, identifies and protects districts, sites, homes, and objects that are relevant to the culture or history of the United States. Once listed in the National Register, a home or site is protected from future demolition and may be eligible for federal funding to be used for renovation or promotion.

THE JOB

The industry of historic preservation received a tremendous boost with the passage of the 1966 National Historic Preservation Act—which gave direction and focus toward the U.S. government's commitment to better care for its historic resources. This law created a need for qualified historians and historic preservationists well trained to identify, preserve, and maintain our national treasures.

Today, historic preservationists can find employment in a variety of settings. Many employed by the federal government work for the National Park Service. The maintenance of battlefields such as Spotsylvania in Virginia, national parks such as the Badlands National Park, and places of interest such as Mount Rushmore are examples of various projects managed by historic preservationists. Their responsibilities may include researching the site's origin, implementing plans of routine maintenance and preservation, and suggesting marketing and educational campaigns to present the site to the public. For example, historic preservationists may suggest plans to help retard erosion in a famous battlefield or prevent pollution of outdoor resources such as Rocky Mountain National Park. They may also conduct research on architectural styles and period-specific décor to properly restore a structure (for example, one of Abraham Lincoln's childhood homes) to its former condition. Many times, a museum is housed alongside a historic site or national park to further educate the public regarding its significance. Preservationists are often employed to help plan the scope of a museum's exhibits and design an educational program for visitors of all ages.

Historic preservationists may also work at the state level. As a result of the 1966 National Preservation Act, each state is required to maintain an office that acts as a liaison for federal and local preservation agencies. State-employed historic preservationists conduct inventories of structures and sites of historic importance, prepare educational programs, and investigate possible National Register nominations. State historical offices are often considered a resource for communities or individuals who may have a particular building or site with historic or cultural relevance. For example, if someone discovered their home once belonged to a prominent person or was designed by a famous architect or was the site of a historic moment, they would turn to their state's historic office. Preservationists would then verify the building's significance and begin the paperwork needed to register the site as a national or state landmark.

Historic preservationists may also work at the local level. Many cities and towns maintain planning commissions or economic development offices to help preserve historic sites or artistic styles within their own communities. For example, when a town experiences a large

The Most Endangered Historic Places in the United States

The National Trust for Historic Preservation, a nonprofit organization committed to saving historic places, publishes an annual list of the most endangered places in the United States. The following places were named as the most endangered in 2006:

- Arts & Industries Building of Smithsonian Institution (Washington, D.C.)
- Blair Mountain Battlefield (Logan County, W. Va.)
- Doo Wop Motels (Wildwood, N.J.)
- Fort Snelling Upper Post (Hennepin County, Minn.)
- Historic Communities and Landmarks of the Mississippi Coast
- Historic Neighborhoods of New Orleans (New Orleans, La.)
- Kenilworth, Ill.
- Kootenai Lodge (Bigfork, Mont.)
- Mission San Miguel Arcangel (San Miguel, Calif.)
- Over-the-Rhine Neighborhood (Cincinnati, Ohio)
- World Trade Center Vesey Street Staircase (New York, N.Y.)

For more information on these and other endangered places, visit http://www.nationaltrust.org.

growth spurt or undergoes a major downtown renovation, planning commissions, alongside historic preservationists, want to ensure that growth is monitored without comprising a neighborhood's important architectural elements or cultural significance. Local volunteers may make up the majority of the staff, but a qualified preservationist is often retained full time to conduct research, create educational programs and tours, and ensure that existing and potential historic sites are maintained within local regulations. Preservationists may also take on many other duties such as performing clerical work, conducting tours, or any other tasks needed to get a project off the ground.

Historic preservationists may also find employment at private firms as full-time employees at larger organizations or at smaller companies as part-time employees or consultants. At this level, preservationists use their training to promote awareness of a community's historical treasures of architecture, art, or natural resources, find sufficient funding from public and/or private sources, and maintain a project within a designated budget.

REQUIREMENTS
High School
Your love of history is a good foundation for a career in preservation. In high school, take as many history classes as possible. Start with U.S. history, but also consider the history of art and architecture. Business classes such as marketing and finance will prove helpful when raising funding for a new project or finishing one within a set budget. As a historic preservationist, you will be expected to write proposals to nominate a potential site, research a specific architectural style, or work as a liaison between federal and local agencies. Begin your training with classes that will strengthen your writing and speaking skills such as speech and English.

Postsecondary Training
More than 55 colleges and universities throughout the United States offer undergraduate or graduate degrees in historic preservation. You'll want to make sure your program of choice is listed with the National Council for Preservation Education (http://www.uvm.edu/histpres/ncpe), which closely monitors programs specializing in this discipline. Most positions, especially those connected with the federal government, require at least a bachelor's degree. Management positions, such as those of staff historian, will require a master's degree or Ph.D.

Expect to take classes that focus on the history of a particular design, such as architecture, landscape, archeology, or urban development.

You will also take classes on the proper techniques of preservation and documentation. Many programs also offer elective classes in law, real estate development, business, government, and design.

Most programs also require successful completion of an internship or apprenticeship. For example, if you choose to intern at the National Park Service, you could acquire valuable field experience working alongside professionals at a variety of locations—a historic site, museum, or national landmark.

Other Requirements

Historic preservationists work on many types of projects, from large government-funded restorations of a city devastated by natural disaster to small grassroots campaign to save a town's Main Street. In turn, preservation professionals must be able to deal with all types of people—from federal officials to ordinary citizens. They must be ready to translate their research in terms easily understood by those outside of the field.

Preservationists must be meticulous with their work, often spending many hours on research, fieldwork, or lobbying various government agencies. Organization and patience are highly valued in this industry.

EXPLORING

Would you like to learn more about the field of historic preservation? You can begin by contacting your local historical society; most towns maintain such an office dedicated to preserving sites and structures within the community. You may be asked to volunteer for a number of tasks ranging from clerical—answering phones, paperwork, mass mailings—to ones that provide you with hands-on experience such as conducting tours of a historical home to gathering signatures for a landmark petition.

Pass on that vacation to a seaside resort and opt instead for a driving tour of the nation's best landmarks. Don't forget to visit museums or tourist centers often located near the sites to learn more about the structure or landmark. Visit the National Trust's Web site (http://www.nationaltrust.org) for its annual list of the country's best destinations and treasures.

EMPLOYERS

The government comprises the largest source of employment for historic preservationists, the majority of which fall under the auspices of the National Park Service. The NPS monitors the work of division offices such as the National Register of Historic Places, the National Historic Landmarks Program, and the Historic American Buildings Survey. Other employment opportunities exist with state and local government agencies, private consulting firms, and nonprofit groups.

STARTING OUT

A college education is required for most jobs in preservation, but work experience is highly valued as well. Most graduates begin their career during an internship as a research assistant for a restoration site or archeology project. Other entry-level jobs at the NPS, for example, include researchers and writers for various educational programs for museums and schools, industry journals, and publications written for the general public.

ADVANCEMENT

Career advancement can be achieved with relevant work experience and additional training. Many preservationists move on to work or manage larger projects within their specific expertise or special interest (say, the Spanish influence in the Southwest or preserving landmarks found along the famous Route 66).

Experienced preservationists may also advance to positions in the private sector. Many businesses such as architectural firms or law firms specializing in the housing market may not be interested in restoration but still desire skilled professionals with knowledge of the National Register. Some preservationists, especially those interested in the legal side of restoration, opt to pursue a law degree specializing in restoration law. Some law schools offer a dual degree in law and a preservation-related field such as urban planning.

EARNINGS

The U.S. Department of Labor does not provide salary information for historic preservationists, but it does report that historians, professionals who perform work often similar to that of preservationists, earned average annual salaries of $44,400 in 2005. Salaries ranged from less than $24,340 to $83,960 or more annually. Historic preservationists typically receive benefits such as medical insurance, paid sick and vacation days, and the opportunity to participate in retirement savings plans.

WORK ENVIRONMENT

Most historic preservationists work in professional office settings, although some have offices at historic sites. They may be required to travel to inspect or gather information at historic sites and other locations. Most preservationists work a standard 40-hour week, but they may work evenings and weekends to attend public hearings with citizens' groups or meet with other professionals.

OUTLOOK

Cities and towns are beginning to recognize the financial, cultural, and historical importance of buildings, structures, natural areas, and other places. As a result, there is an increasing need for historic preservationists. Despite this growth, funding for historic preservation is largely tied to the health of the economy. When the economy is strong, private organizations and government agencies can allot more funds to historic preservation projects. When the economy is weak, there are fewer funds available, and preservation projects, even employment for historic preservationists, may be limited. Those with the most experience and training will have the best prospects.

FOR MORE INFORMATION

For a list of schools granting degrees in historic preservation and available internships, contact
   National Council for Preservation Education
   http://www.ncpe.us

The National Park Service is the umbrella agency for numerous offices devoted to the preservation of historic places. For a list of all federal offices and their liaisons, job opportunities, and available internships, contact
   National Park Service
   1849 C Street, NW
   Washington, DC 20240-0001
   Tel: 202-208-6843
   http://www.nps.gov

For continuing education opportunities and seminars and available scholarships, contact
   National Preservation Institute
   PO Box 1702

Alexandria, VA 22313-1702
Tel: 703-765-0100
Email: info@npi.org
http://www.npi.org

For career and educational opportunities in historic preservation, information on advocacy groups and forums, internship possibilities, and to obtain a copy of the monthly magazine Preservation, *contact*
National Trust for Historic Preservation
1785 Massachusetts Avenue, NW
Washington, DC 20036-2117
Tel: 202-588-6000
http://www.nationaltrust.org

────────── **INTERVIEW** ──────────

Bonnie McDonald is the executive director of the Preservation Alliance of Minnesota, which is headquartered in St. Paul, Minnesota. She talked with the editors of Careers in Focus: Architecture & Building *about her career and the field of historic preservation.*

Q. Please tell us about yourself and your professional background.

A. I discovered my passion for historic preservation in 1997 while attending the University of Minnesota-Twin Cities in pursuit of a bachelor's degree in art history. My studies were focused toward architectural history and historic preservation while pursuing greater understanding of the field. Internships and employment opportunities with the Minneapolis Heritage Preservation Commission, the Preservation Alliance of Minnesota, the State Historic Preservation Office, and the Minnesota Historical Society guided me toward my career in historic preservation advocacy.

After graduating summa cum laude from the University of Minnesota in 1998 with my art history degree, I began pursuing a master's degree in historic preservation planning at Cornell University in 2000. I continued to gain experience by working with Preservation Action in Washington, D.C., and at the Preservation League of New York State. Internships were a crucial part of my education and helped me to build my resume while focusing my efforts.

In 2002, I became the executive director of the Anoka County Historical Society in Anoka, Minnesota, with an aim toward honing my skills in nonprofit administration. I continued to pursue historic preservation as a member of the Midwest Preservation Institute advisory committee and the National Trust for Historic Preservation 2007 Conference steering committee. In November of 2005, the Preservation Alliance of Minnesota hired me as its executive director—fulfilling a dream I had pursued since interning with the organization in 1998.

Q. Please tell us about the work of the Preservation Alliance of Minnesota.

A. The Preservation Alliance of Minnesota (PAM) is the only statewide, private, nonprofit organization advocating the preservation of Minnesota's historic resources. The alliance was incorporated as a 501(c)(3) nonprofit in 1981 by Minnesota citizens concerned about the future of the state's architectural and cultural landmarks. Now celebrating its 25th anniversary, the alliance has grown into a membership network of over 550 dues-paying individuals, businesses, and groups throughout Minnesota, with 80 percent of our members in the Twin Cities metropolitan area. Beyond our membership, we collaborate and partner with other organizations and agencies from the national to the local level. In 2005, through all our programs, publications, and networking, we reached an estimated 2 million Minnesotans.

The formal mission of the alliance is "to preserve, protect, and promote Minnesota's historic resources." The alliance is a growing organization that positions itself at the center of a statewide network of other individuals and organizations. The alliance's mission is achieved when our communities are healthy and vital. Community vitality centers on livable neighborhoods, a thriving economic core, and an educated and engaged public. The preservation of our existing infrastructure, including housing, transportation networks, commercial centers, parks and open space, not only creates viable cities, but it can also be done with relation to all income levels. The alliance exists to educate the public about historic preservation and its community benefits, and to be a source of information, assistance, and inspiration to those who seek to preserve every community's unique sense of place.

Q. Please detail your primary and secondary job duties as executive director.

A. My job as the executive director is to administer all operations of the organization. Operating a nonprofit organization encompasses many areas of expertise. My primary role is to ensure that the organization has adequate financial and human resources and to spend those resources according to the policies and direction set by the board of directors and within our mission. Providing adequate resources takes fundraising. My fundraising activities including meeting individual and corporate donors, soliciting for event sponsorships, writing grants, and trying to engage new members to join the organization.

Secondary to finances is administration, and there is a great deal of administrative work on my everyday schedule. Administrative tasks can include answering phone calls and e-mail, writing letters, getting insurance for a special event, creating our operational budget, drafting organizational policies, and working with volunteers.

I also work very closely with the board of directors and volunteers to accomplish our mission, which is to advocate for historic properties and educate the public about the benefits of historic preservation. We advocate by answering calls from the public and making site visits, writing letters of support, and creating a list of the 10 Most Endangered Historic Places in Minnesota each year. The second part of our mission is education, which requires us to take a more holistic approach. Education is part of everything that we do, so we must be conscious of how we are presenting our programs, our publications, and special events to ensure that the statements are understandable. My job is to make sure that the messages are consistent and well done.

Q. How did your training help you prepare for this career?

A. My training helped me to achieve my dreams earlier than I could ever imagine. At the age of 26, I was already the director of a nonprofit organization, and by 30 I had achieved my dream job. My dream became a reality because of my willingness to take any experience offered to me. In my junior year of college, I offered to volunteer in the conservation laboratory at the Science Museum of Minnesota to gain experience in materials conservation. That volunteer position led to a two-year, paid internship. That experience opened another door, which opened others. By the time I had the required academic background for the position, I also had seven years' experience. Because I was willing to volunteer, work many jobs at one time, and make sacrifices earlier in life, I have a much better future ahead. [I advise those interested in the field of historic preservation to] go after any experience you can as early as you can. Treat your supervisors as mentors and look for learning opportunities. When they see you are eager and willing to learn, they will open doors for you, too.

Q. What are the most important personal and professional qualities for people in historic preservation?

A. Historic preservation is a field that encompasses many topics. To be effective in preserving historic places, one must have basic knowledge—and some interest in—many different disciplines: history; architecture; landscape architecture; archaeology; conservation; construction; materials; land-use policy and law; economics; economic development; and community organizing. It takes creative problem solving to find a solution to challenging preservation issues; therefore, a preservationist needs to be able to work well with others, have patience, and think from many points of view.

Preservation is a challenging field filled with successes, losses, challenges, and controversy. To be successful in preservation, you need to be confident, energetic, and have good communication skills. Research skills are also very valuable. Most important, I believe the best trait is the desire to make a difference with one's life to sustain communities and their uniqueness.

Q. What does the future hold for historic preservation? Is the public becoming more aware of this important field? Is funding more readily available from government and other sources?

A. The field of historic preservation has made great strides since the movement took shape in the 1960s. We now have regulations in place at the local, state, and national level to help protect historic properties as part of the community fabric. There is growing awareness amongst the public for the aesthetic, stabilizing, and economic benefits of preserving historic places. Historic preservationists have made this happen by continuing to bring our message to the public. Heritage tourism, the rise of media focus on historic places (for instance, This Old House and HGTV), and a return to traditional neighborhood design have all influenced how we look at the fabric of our history.

Funding for historic preservation follows the economy. When inflation increases, we see a drop in real estate sales, decreased construction activity, and higher prices for materials needed in a preservation project. This spills over into funding for historic preservation as corporations decrease corporate giving, foundations decrease endowments, the government cuts spending, and individuals spend their dollars on staples rather than donations. We saw this pattern in the 1970s with the energy crisis, in the 1980s with the recession, and during the economic crisis that has followed September 11. However, we are seeing increased economic growth, and that has had a positive effect on preservation. Foundation endowments are on the rise and giving has increased. Corporations are more willing to sponsor activities as their profits grow. Individual giving is on the rise as people become more confident in the future. Government spending has increased some with the positive economic forecast, but current ideology about limiting government spending is hurting preservation activities across the nation.

Interior Designers and Decorators

QUICK FACTS

School Subjects
Art
Business

Personal Skills
Artistic
Communication/ideas

Work Environment
Primarily indoors
Primarily multiple locations

Minimum Education Level
Associate's degree

Salary Range
$23,820 to $41,350 to
$75,860+

Certification or Licensing
Required by certain states

Outlook
About as fast as the average

DOT
141

GOE
01.04.02

NOC
5242

O*NET-SOC
27-1025.00

OVERVIEW

Interior designers and *interior decorators* evaluate, plan, and design the interior areas of residential, commercial, and industrial structures. In addition to helping clients select equipment and fixtures, these professionals supervise the coordination of colors and materials, obtain estimates and costs within the client's budget, and oversee the execution and installation of the project. They also often advise clients on architectural requirements, space planning, and the function and purpose of the environment.

There are currently approximately 65,000 interior designers working in the United States. These specialists are employed by interior design or architectural firms, department stores, furniture stores, hotel chains, and large corporations.

HISTORY

Appreciation for beauty has been expressed in many artforms, including music, painting, sculpture, and poetry. One way to make such beauty a part of everyday life is through decoration of the interiors of buildings. Individuals throughout history have added personal touches of decoration to their homes. Until recently, however, major design and decorating projects have been the privilege of the wealthy.

Artists such as Michelangelo were employed to design and beautify palaces and other buildings, making use of sculpture, paintings, and other wall coverings. Kings sometimes made names for themselves by the decorating trends initiated in their palaces. Such trends came to include furniture, draperies, and often clothing. Home designs and furniture were either largely functional, as in the early American tradition, or extremely ornate, as in the style of Louis XIV of France.

As our society prospered, the field of interior design emerged. While Elsie de Wolfe was the first person to actually practice interior design as a separate profession in 1905, it wasn't until the 1950s that the design revolution really began. Today, design professionals plan interiors of homes, restaurants, hotels, hospitals, theaters, stores, offices, and other buildings.

THE JOB

The terms "interior designer" and "interior decorator" are sometimes used interchangeably. However, there is an important distinction between the two. Interior designers plan and create the overall design for interior spaces, while interior decorators focus on the decorative aspects of the design and furnishing of interiors. A further distinction concerns the type of interior space on which the design or decorating professional works. Specifically, *residential designers* focus on individual homes, while *contract* or *commercial designers* specialize in office buildings, industrial complexes, hotels, hospitals, restaurants, schools, factories, and other nonresidential environments.

Interior designers and decorators perform a wide variety of services, depending on the type of project and the clients' requirements. A job may range from designing and decorating a single room in a private residence to coordinating the entire interior arrangement of a huge building complex. In addition to planning the interiors of new buildings, interior professionals also redesign existing interiors.

Design and decorating specialists begin by evaluating a project. They first consider how the space will be used. In addition to suiting the project's functional requirements, designs must address the needs, desires, tastes, and budget of the client as well. The designer often works closely with the architect in planning the complete layout of rooms and use of space. The designer's plans must work well with the architect's blueprints and comply with other building requirements. Design work of this kind is usually done in connection with the building or renovation of large structures.

Interior professionals may design the furniture and accessories to be used on a project, or they might work with materials that are already available. They select and plan the arrangement of furniture, draperies, floor coverings, wallpaper, paint, and other decorations. They make their decisions only after considering general style, scale of furnishings, colors, patterns, flow, lighting, safety, communication, and a host of other factors. They must also be familiar with local, state, and federal laws as well as building codes and other related regulations.

Although interior designers and decorators may consult with clients throughout the conceptual phase of the design project, they usually make a formal presentation once the design has been formulated. Such presentations may include sketches, scaled floorplans, drawings, models, color charts, photographs of furnishings, and samples of materials for upholstery, draperies, and wall coverings. Designers and decorators also usually provide a cost estimate of furnishings, materials, labor, transportation, and incidentals required to complete the project.

Once plans have been approved by the client, the interior designer and decorator assembles materials—drapery fabrics, upholstery fabrics, new furniture, paint, and wallpaper—and supervises the work, often acting as agent for the client in contracting the services of craftworkers and specifying custom-made merchandise. Interior professionals must be familiar with many materials used in furnishing. They must know when certain materials are suitable, how they will blend with other materials, and how they will wear. They must also be familiar with historical periods influencing design and have a knack for using and combining the best contributions of these designs of the past. Since designers and decorators supervise the work done from their plans, they should know something about painting, carpet laying, carpentry, cabinet making, and other craft areas. In addition, they must be able to buy materials and services at reasonable prices while producing high-quality work.

Some designers and decorators specialize in a particular aspect of interior design, such as furniture, carpeting, or artwork. Others concentrate on particular environments, such as offices, hospitals, restaurants, or transportation, including ships, aircraft, and trains. Still others specialize in the renovation of old buildings. In addition to researching the styles in which rooms were originally decorated and furnished, these workers often supervise the manufacture of furniture and accessories to be used.

Considerable paperwork is involved in interior design and decoration, much of it related to budgets and costs. Interior professionals must determine quantities and make and obtain cost estimates. In addition, designers and decorators write up and administer contracts, obtain permits, place orders, and check deliveries carefully.

All of this work requires an ability to attend to detail in the business aspects of interior design.

REQUIREMENTS

High School

Although formal training is not always necessary in the field of interior design, it is becoming increasingly important and is usually essential for advancement. Most architectural firms, department stores, and design firms accept only professionally trained people, even for beginning positions.

If you're considering a career as an interior designer or decorator, classes in home economics, art history, design, fine arts, and drafting will prove to be valuable. Since interior design is both an art and a business, such courses as marketing, advertising, accounting, management, and general business are important as well.

Postsecondary Training

Professional schools offer two- or three-year certificates or diplomas in interior design. Colleges and universities award undergraduate degrees in four-year programs, and graduate study is also available. The Council for Interior Design Accreditation (CIDA) accredits bachelor's degree programs in interior design. There are more than 145 accredited interior design programs offered through art, architecture, and home economics schools in the United States and Canada. The National Association of Schools of Art and Design also accredits colleges and universities with programs in art and design. College students interested in entering the interior design field should take courses in art history, architectural drawing and drafting, fine arts, furniture design, codes and standards of design, and computer-aided design, as well as classes that focus on the types of materials primarily used, such as fibers, wood, metals, and plastics. Knowledge of lighting and electrical equipment as well as furnishings, art pieces, and antiques, is important.

In addition to art and industry-specific areas of study, courses in business and management are vital to aspiring interior designers and decorators. Learning research methods will help you stay abreast of government regulations and safety standards. You should also have some knowledge of zoning laws, building codes, and other restrictions. Finally, keeping up with product performance and new developments in materials and manufacture is an important part of the ongoing education of the interior designer and decorator.

Art historians, people with architecture or environmental planning experience, and others with qualifications in commercial or industrial design may also qualify for employment in interior design.

Certification or Licensing

Currently, 24 states, the District of Columbia, and Puerto Rico require licensing for interior designers, according to the U.S. Department of Labor. Each of these states has its own requirements for licensing and regulations for practice, so it's important to contact the specific state in order to find out how one can apply. To become eligible for registration or licensing in these jurisdictions, applicants must satisfy experience and education requirements and take the National Council for Interior Design Qualification (NCIDQ) Examination.

To prepare students for this examination, the NCIDQ offers the Interior Design Experience Program. Program participants are required to complete 3,520 hours of documented experience in the following categories: Programming, Schematic Design, Design Development, Contract Documents, Contract Administration, and Professional Practice. According to the council, this experience may be achieved through "working directly in a competency area, by observing others who are engaged in such work, or by attending lectures, seminars, and continuing education courses." Students who have completed at least 96 semester credits hours (or 144 quarter credits hours of education) in a CIDA-accredited interior design program are eligible to participate.

Other Requirements

First and foremost, interior designers and decorators need to have artistic talent, including an eye for color, proportion, balance, and detail, and have the ability to visualize. Designers must be able to render an image clearly and carry it out consistently. At the same time, artistic taste and knowledge of current and enduring fashion trends are essential.

In addition, interior designers need to be able to supervise craftworkers and work well with a variety of other people, including clients and suppliers. Designers should be creative, analytical, and ethical. They also need to be able to focus on the needs of clients, develop a global view, and have an appreciation of diversity. Finally, precision, patience, perseverance, enthusiasm, and attention to detail are vital.

EXPLORING

If you're thinking about becoming an interior designer or decorator, there are several ways to learn about the field. Courses in home economics or any of the fine arts, offered either at school or through a local organization, can give you a taste of some of the areas of knowledge needed by interior designers.

To get a sense of the actual work done by design specialists, you may be able to find a part-time or summer job in a department or furniture store. Such experience will enable you to learn more about the materials used in interior design and decorating and to see the store's interior design service in action. Since the business aspects of interior design are just as important as the creative side, any kind of general selling or business experience will prove to be valuable. As a salesperson at any type of store, for example, you'll learn how to talk to customers, write up orders, close sales, and much more.

In addition to learning about interior design itself, knowledge of auxiliary and support industries will be useful as well. To get a firsthand look at associated fields, you may want to arrange a visit to a construction site, examine an architect's blueprints, talk to someone who specializes in lighting, or tour a furniture manufacturing plant.

Ultimately, the best way to learn about interior design or decorating is to talk to a design professional. While interviewing an interior designer or decorator will be interesting and enlightening, finding a mentor who is doing the type of work that you may want to do in the future is ideal. Such a person can suggest other activities that may be of interest to you as you investigate the interior design field, provide you with the names of trade magazines and/or books that can shed some light on the industry, and serve as a resource for questions you might have.

EMPLOYERS

Approximately 65,000 interior designers and decorators are employed in the United States. Interior designers and decorators can be found wherever there is a need to style or beautify the interior environment of a building. The main professional areas in which they work are residential, government, commercial, retail, hospitality, education and research, health care, and facilities management.

In addition to "traditional" interior design and decorating opportunities, some professionals design theater, film, and television settings. A few designers become teachers, lecturers, or consultants, while others work in advertising and journalism.

The majority of interior designers and decorators work either for themselves or for companies employing fewer than five people. Since the industry is not dominated by giant conglomerates or even midsized firms, employment opportunities are available all across the United States, as well as abroad, in cities both large and small.

STARTING OUT

Most large department stores and design firms with established reputations hire only trained interior designers and decorators. More often than not, these employers look for prospective employees with a good portfolio and a bachelor of fine arts degree. Many schools, however, offer apprenticeship or internship programs in cooperation with professional studios or offices of interior design. These programs make it possible for students to apply their academic training in an actual work environment prior to graduation.

After graduating from a two- or three-year training program (or a four-year university), the beginning interior professional must be prepared to spend one to three years as an assistant to an experienced designer or decorator before achieving full professional status. This is the usual method of entering the field of interior design and gaining membership in a professional organization.

Finding work as an assistant can often be difficult, so be prepared to take any related job. Becoming a sales clerk for interior furnishings, a shopper for accessories or fabrics, or even a receptionist or stockroom assistant can help you get a foot in the door and provide valuable experience as well.

ADVANCEMENT

While advancement possibilities are available, competition for jobs is intense and interior designers and decorators must possess a combination of talent, personality, and business sense to reach the top. Someone just starting out in the field must take a long-range career view, accept jobs that offer practical experience, and put up with long hours and occasionally difficult clients. It usually takes three to six years of practical, on-the-job experience in order to become a fully qualified interior designer or decorator.

As interior professionals gain experience, they can move into positions of greater responsibility and may eventually be promoted to such jobs as design department head or interior furnishings coordinator. Professionals who work with furnishings in architectural firms often become more involved in product design and sales. Designers and decorators can also establish their own businesses. Consulting is another common area of work for the established interior professional.

EARNINGS

Interior designers earned median annual salaries of $41,350 in 2005, according to the U.S. Department of Labor. The highest-paid 10 percent earned more than $75,860, while the lowest-paid 10 percent earned less than $23,820 annually. The U.S. Department of Labor reports the following mean salaries for interior designers by specialty: architectural and engineering services, $49,870; specialized design services, $49,290; and furniture stores, $41,930. In general, interior designers and decorators working in large urban areas make significantly more than those working in smaller cities.

Designers and decorators at interior design firms can earn a straight salary, a salary plus a bonus or commission, or a straight commission. Such firms sometimes pay their employees a percentage of the profits as well. Self-employed professionals may charge an hourly fee, a flat fee, or a combination of the two depending on the project. Some designers and decorators charge a percentage on the cost of materials bought for each project.

The benefits enjoyed by interior designers and decorators, like salaries and bonuses, depend on the particular employer. Benefits may include paid vacations, health and life insurance, paid sick or personal days, employee-sponsored retirement plans, and an employer-sponsored 401(k) program.

WORK ENVIRONMENT

Working conditions for interior designers and decorators vary, depending on where they are employed. While professionals usually have an office or a studio, they may spend the day at a department store, architecture firm, or construction site working with the decorating materials sold by the firm and the clients who have purchased them. In addition, designers often go on-site to consult with and supervise projects being completed by various craftworkers.

Whether designers or decorators are employed by a firm or operate their own businesses, much of their time is spent in clients' homes and businesses. While more and more offices are using the services of interior designers and decorators, the larger part of the business still lies in the area of home design. Residential designers and decorators work intimately with customers, planning, selecting materials, receiving instructions, and sometimes subtly guiding the customers' tastes and choices in order to achieve an atmosphere that is both aesthetic and functional.

While designers and decorators employed by department stores, furniture stores, or design firms often work regular 40-hour weeks, self-employed professionals usually work irregular hours—including evenings and weekends—in order to accommodate their clients' schedules. Deadlines must be met, and if there have been problems and delays on the job, the designer or decorator must work hard to complete the project on schedule. In general, the more successful the individual becomes, the longer and more irregular the hours.

The interior professional's main objective is ultimately to please the customer and thus establish a good reputation. Customers may be difficult at times. They may often change their minds, forcing the designer or decorator to revise plans. Despite difficult clients, the work is interesting and provides a variety of activities.

OUTLOOK

Employment opportunities are expected to be good for interior designers and decorators through 2014, according to the U.S. Department of Labor. However, since the services of design professionals are in many ways a luxury, the job outlook is heavily dependent on the economy. In times of prosperity, there is a steady increase in jobs. When the economy slows down, however, opportunities in the field decrease markedly.

Marketing futurist Faith Popcorn predicts that people will be staying home more (cocooning) and that there will be an increase in what she calls "fantasy adventure." This trend is based on people's desire to stay at home but, at the same time, feel like they are in exotic, remote places. In the future, Popcorn sees homes containing rooms designed like Las Vegas-style resorts, African plains, and other interesting destinations. Both cocooning and fantasy adventure will further add to the many opportunities that will be available to interior designers.

According to the International Interior Design Association's Industry Advisory Council (IAC), a number of trends specific to the industry will also positively influence the employment outlook for interior designers and decorators. Clients in all market areas, for example, will develop an appreciation for the value of interior design work as well as increased respect for the interior professional's expertise. In addition, businesses, ever mindful of their employees' safety, health, and general welfare, will rely more heavily on designers to create interior atmospheres that will positively affect workplace performance.

The IAC also notes the importance of technology in the field of interior design. In addition to affecting the design of homes, technology will impact the production of design materials as well as create the need for multidisciplinary design. Professionals both familiar and comfortable with technology will definitely have an edge in an ever-competitive job market. Finally, the IAC points to the continued importance of education and research in the field of interior design. According to Allison Carll-White, former director of the International Interior Design Association's Research and Education Forum, design organizations will have to offer programs focusing on basic interior design in order to attract talented students to the profession.

While competition for good designing and decorating positions is expected to be fierce, especially for those lacking experience, there is currently a great need for industrial interior designers in housing developments, offices, restaurants, hospital complexes, senior care facilities, hotels, and other large building projects. In addition, as construction of houses increases, there will be many projects available for residential designers and decorators. Designers with strong knowledge of ergonomics and green design will also enjoy excellent job prospects.

FOR MORE INFORMATION

For industry trends, career guidance, and other resources, contact
American Society of Interior Designers
608 Massachusetts Avenue, NE
Washington, DC 20002-6006
Tel: 202-546-3480
http://www.asid.org

For a list of accredited interior design programs, contact
Council for Interior Design Accreditation
146 Monroe Center, NW, Suite 1318
Grand Rapids, MI 49503-2822
Tel: 616-458-0400
Email: info@accredit-id.org
http://www.accredit-id.org

For information on continuing education, publications, and a list of accredited graduate programs in interior design, contact
Interior Design Educators Council
7150 Winton Drive, Suite 300

Indianapolis, IN 46268-4398
Tel: 317-328-4437
Email: info@idec.org
http://www.idec.org

For information on the industry, contact
International Interior Design Association
13-500 Merchandise Mart
Chicago, IL 60654-1104
Tel: 888-799-4432
Email: iidahq@iida.org
http://www.iida.com

For information on accredited interior design programs, contact
National Association of Schools of Art and Design
11250 Roger Bacon Drive, Suite 21
Reston, VA 20190-5248
Tel: 703-437-0700
Email: info@arts-accredit.org
http://nasad.arts-accredit.org

For information on the Interior Design Experience Program, contact
National Council for Interior Design Qualification
1200 18th Street, NW, Suite 1001
Washington, DC 20036-2506
Tel: 202-721-0220
Email: info@ncidq.org
http://www.ncidq.org

For useful information about interior design, visit
Dezignare Interior Design Collective
http://dezignare.com

For useful career information, visit the following Web site
Careers in Interior Design
http://www.careersininteriordesign.com

Landscape Architects

OVERVIEW

Landscape architects plan and design areas such as highways, housing communities, college campuses, commercial centers, recreation facilities, and nature conservation areas. They work to balance beauty and function in developed outdoor areas. There are approximately 25,000 landscape architects employed in the United States.

HISTORY

In the United States, landscape architecture has been practiced as a profession for the last 100 years. During the early part of the 20th century, landscape architects were employed mainly by the wealthy or by the government on public-works projects. In 1918, the practice of dividing large plots of land into individual lots for sale was born. In addition, there was a new public interest in the development of outdoor recreational facilities. These two factors provided many new opportunities for landscape architects.

The most dramatic growth occurred following the environmental movement of the 1960s, when public respect for protection of valuable natural resources reached an all-time high. Landscape architects have played a key role in encouraging the protection of natural resources while providing for the increasing housing and recreation needs of the American public.

In the last 30 years, the development of recreational areas has become more important, as has the development of streets, bypasses, and massive highways. Landscape architects are needed in most projects of this nature. Both developers and community planners draw upon the services of landscape architects now more than ever.

THE JOB

Landscape architects plan and design outdoor spaces that make the best use of the land and at the same time respect the needs of the natural environment. They may be involved in a number of different types of projects, including the design of parks or gardens, scenic roads, housing projects, college or high school campuses, country clubs, cemeteries, or golf courses. They are employed by both the public and private sectors.

Landscape architects begin a project by carefully reviewing their client's desires, including the purpose, structures needed, and funds available. They study the work site itself, observing and mapping such features as the slope of the land, existing structures, plants, and trees. They also consider different views of the location, taking note of shady and sunny areas, the structure of the soil, and existing utilities.

Landscape architects consult with a number of different people, such as engineers, architects, city officials, zoning experts, real estate agents and brokers, and landscape nursery workers to develop a complete understanding of the job. Then they develop detailed plans and drawings of the site to present to the client for approval. Some projects take many months before the proposed plans are ready to be presented to the client.

After developing final plans and drawing up a materials list, landscape architects invite construction companies to submit bids for the job. Depending upon the nature of the project and the contractual agreement, landscape architects may remain on the job to supervise construction, or they may leave the project once work has begun. Those who remain on the job serve as the client's representative until the job is completed and approved.

REQUIREMENTS

High School

To prepare for a college program in landscape architecture, you should take courses in English composition and literature; social sciences, including history, government, and sociology; natural sciences, including biology, chemistry, and physics; and mathematics. If available, take drafting and mechanical drawing courses to begin building the technical skills needed for the career.

Postsecondary Training

A bachelor's or master's degree in landscape architecture is usually the minimum requirement for entry into this field. Undergraduate and graduate programs in landscape architecture are offered in various colleges and universities. Seventy-seven programs at 59 colleges and universities are accredited by the Landscape Architectural Accreditation Board of the American Society of Landscape Architects (ASLA). Courses of study usually focus on six basic areas of the profession: landscape design, landscape construction, plants, architecture, graphic expression (mechanical, freehand, and computer-based drawings), and verbal expression.

Hands-on work is a crucial element to the curriculum. Whenever possible, students work on real projects to gain experience with computer-aided design programs and video simulation.

Certification or Licensing
Almost all states require landscape architects to be licensed. To obtain licensure, applicants must pass the Landscape Architect Registration Examination, sponsored by the Council of Landscape Architectural Registration Boards (CLARB). Though standards vary by state, most require applicants to have a degree from an accredited program and to be working toward one to four years of experience in the field. In addition, 14 states require prospective landscape architects to pass another exam that tests knowledge of local environmental regulations, vegetation, and other characteristics unique to the particular state. Because these standards vary, landscape architects may have to reapply for licensure if they plan to work in a different state. However, in many cases, workers who meet the national standards and have passed the exam may be granted the right to work elsewhere. For more information on licensing, contact the CLARB (http://www.clarb.org) or the ASLA (http://www.asla.org).

Landscape architects working for the federal government need a bachelor's or master's degree but do not need to be licensed.

Other Requirements
You should be interested in art and nature and have good business sense, especially if you hope to work independently. Interest in environmental protection, community improvement, and landscape design is also crucial for the profession. You should also be flexible and be able to think creatively to solve unexpected problems that may develop during the course of a project.

EXPLORING

If you are interested in learning more about the field, you can gather information and experience in a number of ways. Apply for a summer internship with a landscape architectural firm or at least arrange to talk with someone in the field. Ask them questions about their daily duties, the job's advantages and disadvantages, and if they recommend any landscape architecture programs. Finally, you can take the Landscape Architecture Interest Test at the Web site (http://www.asla.org/nonmembers/recruitment/lainttest.htm) of the American Society of Landscape Architects to gauge your interest in the field.

EMPLOYERS

There are roughly 25,000 landscape architects employed in the United States. Landscape architects are found in every state in the United States, in small towns and cities as well as heavily populated areas. Some work in rural areas, such as those who plan and design parks and recreational areas. However, the majority of positions are found in suburban and urban areas.

Landscape architects work for a variety of different employers in both the public and private sectors. They may work with a school board planning a new elementary or high school, with manufacturers developing a new factory, with homeowners improving the land surrounding their home, or with a city council planning a new suburban development.

In the private sector, most landscape architects do some residential work, though few limit themselves entirely to projects with individual homeowners. Larger commercial or community projects are usually more profitable. Workers in the public sector plan and design government buildings, parks, and public lands. They also may conduct studies on environmental issues and restore lands such as mines or landfills.

STARTING OUT

After graduating from a landscape architecture program, you can usually receive job assistance from the school's career placement service. Although these services do not guarantee a job, they can be of great help in making initial contacts. Many positions are posted by the American Society of Landscape Architects and published in its two journals, *Landscape Architectural News Digest Online* (http://www.asla.org/members/land) and *Landscape Architecture* (http://www.asla.org/nonmembers/lam.cfm). Government positions are normally filled through civil service examinations. Information regarding vacancies may be obtained through the local, state, or federal civil service commissions.

Most new hires are often referred to as interns or apprentices until they have gained initial experience in the field and have passed the necessary examinations. Apprentices' duties vary by employer; some handle background project research, others are directly involved in planning and design. Whatever their involvement, all new hires work under the direct supervision of a licensed landscape architect. All drawings and plans must be signed and sealed by the licensed supervisor for legal purposes.

ADVANCEMENT

After obtaining licensure and gaining work experience in all phases of a project's development, landscape architects can become project managers, responsible for overseeing the entire project and meeting schedule deadlines and budgets. They can also advance to the level of associate, increasing their earning opportunities by gaining a profitable stake in a firm.

The ultimate objective of many landscape architects is to gain the experience necessary to organize and open their own firm. According to the U.S. Department of Labor, approximately 26 percent of all landscape architects are self-employed—more than three times the average of workers in other professions. After the initial investment in computer-aided design software, few start-up costs are involved in breaking into the business independently.

EARNINGS

Salaries for landscape architects vary depending on the employer, work experience, location, and whether they are paid a straight salary or earn a percentage of a firm's profits.

According to 2005 data from the U.S. Department of Labor, the median annual salary for landscape architects was $54,220. The lowest-paid 10 percent earned less than $33,570 and the highest-paid 10 percent earned more than $92,310. The average salary for those working in architectural and engineering services was $59,470 in 2005.

Benefits also vary depending on the employer but usually include health insurance coverage, paid vacation time, and sick leave. Many landscape architects work for small landscaping firms or are self-employed. These workers generally receive fewer benefits than those who work for large organizations.

WORK ENVIRONMENT

Landscape architects spend much of their time in the field gathering information at the work site. They also spend time in the office, drafting plans and designs. Those working for larger organizations may have to travel farther away to worksites.

Work hours are generally regular, except during periods of increased business or when nearing a project deadline. Hours vary for self-employed workers because they determine their own schedules.

OUTLOOK

According to the *Occupational Outlook Handbook*, the employment of landscape architects is expected to increase faster than the average for all occupations through 201. The increase in demand for landscape architects is a result of several factors: a boom in the construction industry, the need to refurbish existing sites, and the increase in city and environmental planning and historic preservation. In addition, many job openings are expected to result from the need to replace experienced workers who leave the field.

The need for landscape architecture depends to a great extent on the construction industry. In the event of an economic downturn, when real estate transactions and the construction business are expected to drop off, opportunities for landscape architects will also dwindle.

Opportunities will be the greatest for workers who develop strong technical skills. The growing use of technology such as computer-aided design will not diminish the demand for landscape architects. New and improved techniques will be used to create better designs more efficiently rather than reduce the number of workers needed to do the job.

FOR MORE INFORMATION

For information on the career, accredited education programs, licensure requirements, and available publications, contact
American Society of Landscape Architects
636 Eye Street, NW
Washington, DC 20001-3736
Tel: 202-898-2444
http://www.asla.org

For information on student resources, license examinations, and continuing education, contact

Council of Landscape Architectural Registration Boards
144 Church Street, NW, Suite 201
Vienna, VA 22180-4550
Tel: 703-319-8380
Email: Info@Clarb.org
http://www.clarb.org

For career and educational information, visit the following Web site sponsored by the Landscape Architecture Foundation.

LAprofession.org
http://www.laprofession.org

────── INTERVIEW ──────

Dennis Carmichael is a vice president at EDAW, a company that specializes in landscape architecture, planning/urban design, and environmental design. Dennis has a bachelor's of landscape architecture from SUNY College of Environmental Science and Forestry. He has worked for EDAW for 25 years. Dennis talked with the editors of Careers in Focus: Architecture & Building *about his career and the field of landscape design.*

Q. Please briefly describe your primary and secondary job duties as a landscape architect.

A. My primary role is to lead design projects for parks, plazas, and planned communities. As a vice president, I also have to win new contracts for projects to sustain the business and also mentor young people in the office so they can grow into strong professionals themselves. While I spend some time drawing plans, the majority of my time is spent in presenting ideas to clients, reviewing and critiquing design work by my staff, and nurturing new clients.

Q. How/where did you get your first job in this field? What did you do?

A. I got my first job in a small office in New York City. I decided that was where I wanted to work and interviewed with a series of firms there. I received two offers and chose the firm because of the type and quality of design work they did. I learned a terrific amount about construction technology by spending my time there producing contract documents (blueprints) under the direction of the three partners. They instilled in me the sense that no detail was unimportant and that everything was connected to a larger idea, concepts I teach to others today.

Q. What are the most important personal and professional qualities for landscape architects?

A. The most important personal quality for landscape architects is to believe that they can make a positive difference in the quality of our environment. Every decision a landscape architect makes, large and small, can improve our world through better air quality, cleaner water, or safer streets. Landscape architects have to be guided by that faith from within that they can leave a place better than they found it, for the betterment of society. The most important professional quality is to be a good communicator, both in listening to the needs of clients and users of landscapes and also in articulating ideas and concepts so that people may understand and appreciate them. While drawing skills are important, communication of those creative ideas is even more important to successfully implementing them.

Q. What are some of the pros and cons of your job?

A. The life of a landscape architect is rich with experience including visiting project sites, brainstorming bold ideas, creating beautiful drawings, and interacting with dynamic people. It is always exciting because there are always new projects, new clients, and new ideas to pursue. What is most rewarding is to see your work built, as seeing an idea on paper come to life and be used and appreciated by others is a real thrill. There are downsides to the profession. You do not win every commission you seek. The clients do not have infinite budgets and sometimes projects do not turn out as envisioned. Sometimes projects are built and then poorly maintained, so they deteriorate. Patience is a virtue for landscape architects because projects take time to design and build, and then landscape itself takes time to mature.

Q. What advice would you offer students as they graduate and look for jobs in this field?

A. The most important advice I would give a recent graduate landscape architect is to remember that the work we do is not cosmetic, but more fundamental to a healthy environment. There is a perception that landscape architects simply add plants to an area to make it more attractive. The truth is, landscape architects envision exterior environments for work, play, and education that add value to society by protecting natural resources, enhancing air and water quality, and creating places for people to come together as a community. These values are much deeper than cosmetic and more sustainable over time as well.

Q. What is the future employment outlook for landscape architects?

A. The outlook for employment in the field of landscape architecture is very bright. Each year, more jobs are created than graduates of landscape architecture programs. Most Americans consider themselves environmentalists, and these values will only increase over the next few decades as urban sprawl, global warming, forest depletion, and water scarcities create demand for the wise planning of our land. Landscape architects are well positioned to be leaders in the solutions to these pressing problems as they are skilled in the arts, sciences, and public communication. I believe the profession will continue to grow both in numbers and in influence over the next few decades.

Office Clerks

QUICK FACTS

School Subjects
Business
English
Mathematics

Personal Skills
Communication/ideas
Following instructions

Work Environment
Primarily indoors
Primarily one location

Minimum Education Level
High school diploma

Salary Range
$14,530 to $22,776 to
$36,460+

Certification or Licensing
None available

Outlook
More slowly than the
average

DOT
209

GOE
07.07.03

NOC
1411

O*NET-SOC
43-9061.00

OVERVIEW

Office clerks employed in the construction and architecture industries perform a variety of clerical tasks that help an office run smoothly, including file maintenance, mail sorting, and record-keeping. In large companies, office clerks might have specialized tasks such as inputting data into a computer, but in most cases, clerks are flexible and have many duties including typing, answering telephones, taking messages, making photocopies, and preparing mailings. Office clerks usually work under close supervision, often with experienced clerks directing their activities. There are approximately 667,000 office and administrative support workers employed in the construction industry.

HISTORY

Before the 18th century, many businesspeople did their own office work, such as shipping products, accepting payments, and recording inventory. The industrial revolution changed the nature of business by popularizing the specialization of labor, which allowed companies to increase their output dramatically. At this time, office clerks were brought in to handle the growing number of clerical duties.

Office workers have become more important as computers, word processors, and other technological advances have increased both the volume of business information available and the speed with which administrative decisions can be made. The number of office workers in the United States has grown as more trained personnel are needed to handle the volume of business communication and information. Businesses (such as architectural firms, construction companies, and engineering firms) and government agencies depend on skilled office workers to file and sort documents, operate office equipment, and cooperate with others to ensure the flow of information.

THE JOB

Office clerks usually perform a variety of tasks as part of their overall job responsibility. They may type or file bills, statements, and business correspondence. They may stuff envelopes, answer telephones, and sort mail. Office clerks also enter data into computer databases, run errands, and operate office equipment such as photocopiers, fax machines, and switchboards. In the course of an average day, an office clerk usually performs a combination of these and other clerical tasks, spending an hour or so on one task and then moving on to another as directed by an office manager or other supervisor.

An office clerk may work with other office personnel, such as a bookkeeper or accountant, to maintain a company's financial records. The clerk may type and mail invoices and sort payments as they come in, keep payroll records, or take inventories. With more

Facts About the Construction Industry

- There are about 8.9 million people employed in the U.S. construction industry—7 million in wage and salary jobs and 1.9 million who are self-employed and unpaid family workers.
- There are approximately 818,000 construction businesses in the United States: 247,000 are building construction contractors; 57,000 are heavy and civil engineering construction or highway contractors; and 514,000 are specialty trade contractors.
- Approximately 20 percent of workers in the construction industry work more than 45 hours per week.
- About 17 percent of construction trade workers are members of a union or covered by union contracts—a percentage slightly higher than the average for all workers in private industry.
- Employment in the construction industry is expected to grow by 11 percent through 2014—slightly less than the average for all industries.

Source: U.S. Department of Labor

experience, the clerk may be asked to update customer files to reflect receipt of payments and verify records for accuracy.

Office clerks often deliver messages from one office worker to another, an especially important responsibility in larger companies. In addition, clerks may relay questions and answers from one department head to another. Similarly, clerks may relay messages from people outside the company or employees who are outside of the office to those working in house. Office clerks may also work with other personnel on individual projects, such as preparing a yearly budget or making sure a mass mailing gets out on time.

Administrative clerks assist in the efficient operation of an office by compiling business records; providing information to sales personnel and customers; and preparing and sending out bills, policies, invoices, and other business correspondence. Administrative clerks may also keep financial records and prepare the payroll. *File clerks* review and classify letters, documents, articles, and other information and then file this material so it can be quickly retrieved at a later time. They contribute to the smooth distribution of information at a company.

REQUIREMENTS

High School
To prepare for a career as an office clerk, you should take courses in English, mathematics, and as many business-related subjects, such as keyboarding and bookkeeping, as possible. Community colleges and vocational schools often offer business education courses that provide training for general office workers.

Postsecondary Training
A high school diploma is usually sufficient for beginning office clerks, although business courses covering office machine operation and bookkeeping are also helpful. If you plan on working as a clerk in the construction, real estate, or construction industries, it is a good idea to take some entry-level courses in these areas at a two-year college to improve your knowledge of the field. To succeed in this field, you should have computer skills, the ability to concentrate for long periods of time on repetitive tasks, good English and communication skills, and mathematical abilities. Legible handwriting is also a necessity.

Other Requirements
To find work as an office clerk, you should have an even temperament, strong communication skills, and the ability to work well with

others. You should find systematic and detailed work appealing. Other personal qualifications include dependability, trustworthiness, and a neat personal appearance.

EXPLORING

You can gain experience by taking on clerical or bookkeeping responsibilities with a school club or other organization. In addition, some school work-study programs may provide opportunities for part-time on-the-job training with local businesses. You may also be able to get a part-time or summer job in a construction office by contacting businesses directly or enlisting the aid of a guidance counselor. Training in the operation of business machinery (computers, word processors, and so on) may be available through evening courses offered by business schools and community colleges.

EMPLOYERS

Approximately 667,000 office and administrative support workers are employed in the construction industry, but office clerks work in almost any industry imaginable.

Employers include architectural and engineering firms; historic preservation agencies and organizations; local government; health care and social assistance organizations; administrative and support services companies; finance and insurance companies; or professional, scientific, and technical services industries. Smaller companies also hire office workers and sometimes offer greater opportunities to gain experience in a variety of clerical tasks.

STARTING OUT

To secure an entry-level position, you should contact businesses or government agencies directly. Newspaper ads and temporary-work agencies are also good sources for finding jobs in this area. Most companies provide on-the-job training, during which company policies and procedures are explained.

ADVANCEMENT

Office clerks usually begin their employment performing more routine tasks such as delivering messages and sorting and filing mail. With experience, they may advance to more complicated assignments and assume a greater responsibility for the entire project to be completed. Those who demonstrate the desire and ability may move to other clerical positions, such as secretary or receptionist. Clerks with good leadership skills may become group managers or supervisors. To be promoted to a professional occupation such as accountant, a college degree or other specialized training is usually necessary.

The high turnover rate that exists among office clerks increases promotional opportunities. The number and kind of opportunities, however, usually depend on the place of employment and the ability, education, and experience of the employee.

EARNINGS

Salaries for office clerks vary depending on the size and geographic location of the company and the skills of the worker. According to the U.S. Department of Labor, the mean salary for full-time office clerks employed in the construction industry was $22,776 in 2005. The lowest-paid 10 percent of all office clerks earned less than $14,530, while the highest paid group earned more than $36,460.

Full-time workers generally also receive paid vacations, health insurance, sick leave, and other benefits.

WORK ENVIRONMENT

As is the case with most office workers, office clerks work an average 37- to 40-hour week. They usually work in comfortable surroundings and are provided with modern equipment. Although clerks have a variety of tasks and responsibilities, the job itself can be fairly routine and repetitive. Clerks often interact with accountants and other office personnel and may work under close supervision.

OUTLOOK

Although employment of office clerks is expected to grow more slowly than the average through 2014, there will still be many jobs available due to the vastness of this field and a high turnover rate. With the increased use of data-processing equipment and other types of automated office machinery, more and more employers are hiring people proficient in a variety of office tasks. According to OfficeTeam, the following industries show the strongest demand for qualified administrative staff: health care, mortgage and title, and nonprofits. Other industries that provide good opportunities include construction, technology, and transportation.

Because they are so versatile, office workers can find employment in virtually any kind of industry, so their overall employment does not depend on the fortunes of any single sector of the economy. In addition to private companies, the federal government should continue to be a good source of jobs. Employment opportunities should be especially good for those trained in various computer skills as well as other office machinery. Temporary and part-time work opportunities should also increase, especially during busy business periods.

FOR MORE INFORMATION

For information on seminars, conferences, and news on the industry, contact

National Association of Executive Secretaries and Administrative Assistants
900 South Washington Street, Suite G-13
Falls Church, VA 22046-4009
Tel: 703-237-8616
Email: Headquarters@naesaa.com
http://www.naesaa.com

Visit the following Web site for information on careers in construction:
Construct My Future
http://www.constructmyfuture.com

For free office career and salary information and job listings, visit the following Web site:
OfficeTeam
http://www.officeteam.com

Plumbers and Pipefitters

QUICK FACTS

School Subjects
Chemistry
Physics

Personal Skills
Following instructions
Mechanical/manipulative

Work Environment
Primarily indoors
Primarily multiple locations

Minimum Education Level
Apprenticeship

Salary Range
$24,730 to $42,160 to
$70,360+

Certification or Licensing
Required by certain states

Outlook
About as fast as the average

DOT
862

GOE
05.05.03

NOC
7251

O*NET-SOC
47-2152.00, 47-2152.01,
47-2152.02

OVERVIEW

Plumbers and pipefitters assemble, install, alter, and repair pipes and pipe systems that carry water, steam, air, or other liquids and gases for sanitation and industrial purposes as well as other uses. Plumbers also install plumbing fixtures, appliances, and heating and refrigerating units. There are approximately 561,000 plumbers and pipefitters working in the United States.

HISTORY

Although the early Egyptians are known to have used lead pipes to carry water and drainage into and out of buildings, the use of plumbing in a citywide system was first achieved in the Roman Empire. In Renaissance times, the techniques of plumbing were revived and used in some of the great castles and monasteries. But the greatest advances in plumbing were made in the 19th century, when towns grew into cities and the need for adequate public sanitation was recognized.

THE JOB

Because little difference exists between the work of the plumber and the pipefitter in most cases, the two are often considered to be one trade. However, some craftsworkers specialize in one field or the other, especially in large cities.

The work of pipefitters differs from that of plumbers mainly in its location and the variety and size of pipes used. Plumbers work

A pipefitter repairs a pipe in a manufacturing plant. *(Index Stock Imagery)*

primarily in residential and commercial buildings, whereas pipefitters are generally employed by large industrial concerns—such as oil refineries, refrigeration plants, and defense establishments—where more complex systems of piping are used. Plumbers assemble, install, and repair heating, water, and drainage systems, especially those that must be connected to public utilities systems. Some of their jobs include replacing burst pipes and installing and repairing sinks, bathtubs, water heaters, hot water tanks, garbage disposal units, dishwashers, and water softeners. Plumbers also may work on septic tanks, cesspools, and sewers. During the final construction stages of both commercial and residential buildings, plumbers install heating and air-conditioning units and connect radiators, water heaters, and plumbing fixtures.

Most plumbers follow set procedures in their work. After inspecting the installation site to determine pipe location, they cut and thread pipes, bend them to required angles by hand or machines, and then join them by means of welded, brazed, caulked, soldered, or threaded joints. To test for leaks in the system, they fill the pipes with water or air. Plumbers use a variety of tools, including hand tools such as wrenches, reamers, drills, braces and bits, hammers, chisels, and saws; power machines that cut, bend, and thread pipes; gasoline torches; and welding, soldering, and brazing equipment.

Specialists include diesel engine pipefitters, steamfitters, ship- and boat-building coppersmiths, industrial-gas fitters, gas-main fitters, prefab plumbers, and pipe cutters.

REQUIREMENTS

High School

A high school diploma is especially important for getting into a good apprenticeship program. High school preparation should include courses in mathematics, chemistry, and physics, as well as some shop courses.

Postsecondary Training

To qualify as a plumber, a person must complete either a formal apprenticeship or an informal on-the-job training program. To be considered for the apprenticeship program, individuals must pass an examination administered by the state employment agency and have their qualifications approved by the local joint labor-management apprenticeship committee.

The apprenticeship program for plumbers consists of four years of carefully planned activity combining direct training with at least 144 hours of formal classroom instruction each year. The program is designed to give apprentices diversified training by having them work for several different plumbing or pipefitting contractors.

On-the-job training, on the other hand, usually consists of working for five or more years under the guidance of an experienced craftsworker. Trainees begin as helpers until they acquire the necessary skills and knowledge for more difficult jobs. Frequently, they supplement this practical training by taking trade (or correspondence) courses.

Certification or Licensing

A license is required for plumbers in many places. To obtain this license, plumbers must pass a special examination to demonstrate their knowledge of local building codes as well as their all-around knowledge of the trade. To become a plumbing contractor in most places, a master plumber's license must be obtained.

Other Requirements

To be successful in this field, you should like to solve a variety of problems and should not object to being called on during evenings, weekends, or holidays to perform emergency repairs. As in most service occupations, plumbers should be able to get along well with all kinds of people. You should be a person who works well alone but who can also direct the work of helpers and enjoy the company of those in the other construction trades.

EXPLORING

Although opportunities for direct experience in this occupation are rare for those in high school, there are ways to explore the field. Speaking to an experienced plumber or pipefitter will give you a clearer picture of day-to-day work in this field. Pursuing hobbies with mechanical aspects will help you determine how much you like such hands-on work.

EMPLOYERS

Plumbers and pipefitters hold about 561,000 jobs. Approximately 50 percent work for mechanical and plumbing contractors engaged in new construction, repair, modernization, or maintenance work. One in 10 plumbers and pipefitters are self-employed.

STARTING OUT

Applicants who wish to become apprentices usually contact local plumbing, heating, and air-conditioning contractors who employ plumbers, the state employment service bureau, or the local branch of the United Association of Journeymen and Apprentices of the Plumbing and Pipefitting Industry of the United States and Canada. Individual contractors or contractor associations often sponsor local apprenticeship programs. Apprentices very commonly go on to permanent employment with the firms with which they apprenticed.

ADVANCEMENT

If plumbers have certain qualities such as the ability to deal with people and good judgment and planning skills, they may progress to such positions as supervisor or job estimator for plumbing or pipefitting contractors. If they work for large industrial companies, they may advance to the position of job superintendent. Many plumbers go into business for themselves. Eventually, they may expand their activities and become contractors, employing other workers.

EARNINGS

Plumbers and pipefitters had median earnings of $42,160 in 2005, according to the U.S. Department of Labor. Wages ranged from less than $24,730 to $70,360 or more. Pay rates for apprentices usually start at 50 percent of the experienced worker's rate and increase by five percent every six months until a rate of 95 percent is reached. Benefits for union workers usually include health insurance, sick time, and vacation pay, as well as pension plans.

WORK ENVIRONMENT

Most plumbers have a regular 40-hour workweek with extra pay for overtime. Unlike most of the other building trades, this field is little affected by seasonal factors. The work of the plumber is active and strenuous. Standing for prolonged periods and working in cramped or uncomfortable positions are often necessary. Possible risks include falls from ladders, cuts from sharp tools, and burns from hot pipes or steam. Working with clogged pipes and toilets can also be smelly.

OUTLOOK

Employment opportunities for plumbers are expected to grow about as fast as the average for all jobs through 2014, according to the U.S. Department of Labor. The department predicts excellent opportunities for plumbers and pipefitters due to a shortage of workers entering the field and a projected wave of retirements in the next decade. Construction projects are usually only short-term in nature and more plumbers will find steady work in renovation, repair, and maintenance. Since pipework is becoming more important in large industries, more workers will be needed for installation and maintenance work, especially where refrigeration and air-conditioning equipment is used. Employment opportunities fluctuate with local economic conditions, although the plumbing industry is less affected by economic trends than other construction trades.

FOR MORE INFORMATION

For more information about becoming a plumber or pipefitter, contact the following organizations:

Plumbing-Heating-Cooling Contractors Association
180 South Washington Street
PO Box 6808

Falls Church, VA 22046-2900
Tel: 800-533-7694
Email: naphcc@naphcc.org
http://www.phccweb.org

United Association of Journeymen and Apprentices of the Plumbing and Pipefitting Industry of the United States and Canada
901 Massachusetts Avenue, NW
Washington, DC 20001-4397
Tel: 202-628-5823
http://www.ua.org

For information on state apprenticeship programs, visit
Employment & Training Administration
U.S. Department of Labor
http://www.doleta.gov

Surveyors

OVERVIEW

Surveyors mark exact measurements and locations of elevations, points, lines, and contours on or near Earth's surface. They measure distances between points to determine property boundaries and to provide data for mapmaking, construction projects, and other engineering purposes. There are approximately 56,000 surveyors employed in the United States.

HISTORY

As the United States expanded from the Atlantic to the Pacific, people moved over the mountains and plains into the uncharted regions of the West. They found it necessary to chart their routes and to mark property lines and borderlines by surveying and filing claims.

The need for accurate geographical measurements and precise records of those measurements has increased over the years. Surveying measurements are needed for the location of a trail, highway, or road; the site of a log cabin, frame house, or skyscraper; the right-of-way for water pipes, drainage ditches, and telephone lines; and for the charting of unexplored regions, bodies of water, land, and underground mines.

As a result, the demand for professional surveyors has grown and become more complex. New computerized systems are now used to map, store, and retrieve geographical data more accurately and efficiently. This new technology has not only improved the process of surveying but extended its reach as well. Surveyors can now make detailed maps of ocean floors and the moon's surface.

THE JOB

On proposed construction projects such as highways, airstrips, and housing developments, it is the surveyor's responsibility to make necessary measurements through an accurate and detailed survey of the area. The surveyor usually works with a field party consisting of several people. *Instrument assistants,* called *surveying and mapping technicians,* handle a variety of surveying instruments including the theodolite, transit, level, surveyor's chain, rod, and other electronic equipment. In the course of the survey, it is important that all readings be recorded accurately and field notes maintained so that the survey can be checked for accuracy.

Surveyors may specialize in one or more particular types of surveying.

Land surveyors establish township, property, and other tract-of-land boundary lines. Using maps, notes, or actual land title deeds, they survey the land, checking for the accuracy of existing records. This information is used to prepare legal documents such as deeds and leases. *Land surveying managers* coordinate the work of surveyors, their parties, and legal, engineering, architectural, and other staff involved in a project. In addition, these managers develop policy, prepare budgets, certify work upon completion, and handle numerous other administrative duties.

Highway surveyors establish grades, lines, and other points of reference for highway construction projects. This survey information is essential to the work of the numerous engineers and the construction crews who build the new highway.

Geodetic surveyors measure large masses of land, sea, and space that must take into account the curvature of Earth and its geophysical characteristics. Their work is helpful in establishing points of reference for smaller land surveys, determining national boundaries, and preparing maps. *Geodetic computers* calculate latitude, longitude, angles, areas, and other information needed for mapmaking. They work from field notes made by an engineering survey party and also use reference tables and a calculating machine or computer.

Marine surveyors measure harbors, rivers, and other bodies of water. They determine the depth of the water through measuring sound waves in relation to nearby land masses. Their work is essential for planning and constructing navigation projects, such as breakwaters, dams, piers, marinas, and bridges, and for preparing nautical charts and maps.

Mine surveyors make surface and underground surveys, preparing maps of mines and mining operations. Such maps are helpful in

Surveyors must be able to visualize and understand objects in two and three dimensions. *(Index Stock Imagery)*

examining underground passages within the levels of a mine and assessing the volume and location of raw material available.

Geophysical prospecting surveyors locate and mark sites considered likely to contain petroleum deposits. *Oil-well directional surveyors* use sonic, electronic, and nuclear measuring instruments to gauge the presence and amount of oil- and gas-bearing reservoirs. *Pipeline surveyors* determine rights-of-way for oil construction projects, providing information essential to the preparation for and laying of the lines.

Photogrammetric engineers determine the contour of an area to show elevations and depressions and indicate such features as mountains, lakes, rivers, forests, roads, farms, buildings, and other landmarks. Aerial, land, and water photographs are taken with special equipment able to capture images of very large areas. From these pictures, accurate measurements of the terrain and surface features can be made. These surveys are helpful in construction projects and in the preparation of topographical maps. Photogrammetry is particularly helpful in charting areas that are inaccessible or difficult to travel.

REQUIREMENTS

High School
Does this work interest you? If so, you should prepare for it by taking plenty of math and science courses in high school. Take algebra,

geometry, and trigonometry to become comfortable making different calculations. Earth science, chemistry, and physics classes should also be helpful. Geography will help you learn about different locations and their characteristics. Benefits from taking mechanical drawing and other drafting classes include an increased ability to visualize abstractions, exposure to detailed work, and an understanding of perspectives. Taking computer science classes will prepare you for working with technical surveying equipment.

Postsecondary Training
Depending on state requirements, you will need some postsecondary education. The quickest route is by earning a bachelor's degree in surveying or engineering combined with on-the-job training. Other entry options include obtaining more job experience combined with a one- to three-year program in surveying and surveying technology offered by community colleges, technical institutes, and vocational schools.

Certification or Licensing
The American Congress on Surveying and Mapping (ACSM) has partnered with the Federal Emergency Management Agency to create a certification program for floodplain surveyors. Contact the ACSM for details on the program.

All 50 states require that surveyors making property and boundary surveys be licensed or registered. The requirements for licensure vary, but most require a degree in surveying or a related field, a certain number of years of experience, and passing of examinations in land surveying. Generally, the higher the degree obtained, the less experience required. Those with bachelor's degrees may need only two to four years of on-the-job experience, while those with a lesser degree may need up to 12 years of experience to obtain a license. Information on specific requirements can be obtained by contacting the licensure department of the state in which you plan to work. If you are seeking employment in the federal government, you must take a civil service examination and meet the educational, experience, and other specified requirements for the position.

Other Requirements
The ability to work with numbers and perform mathematical computations accurately and quickly is very important. Other helpful qualities are the ability to visualize and understand objects in two and three dimensions (spatial relationships) and the ability to discriminate between and compare shapes, sizes, lines, shadings, and other forms (form perception).

Surveyors walk a great deal and carry equipment over various types of terrain, so endurance and coordination are important physical assets. In addition, surveyors direct and supervise the work of their team, so you should be good at working with other people and demonstrate leadership ability.

EXPLORING

While you are in high school, begin to familiarize yourself with terms, projects, and tools used in this profession by reading books and magazines on the topic. One magazine you can take a look at online is *Professional Surveyor Magazine* at http://www.profsurv. com. One of the best opportunities for experience is a summer job with a construction outfit or company that requires survey work. Even if the job does not involve direct contact with survey crews, it will offer an opportunity to observe surveyors and talk with them about their work.

Some colleges have work-study programs that offer on-the-job experience. These opportunities, like summer or part-time jobs, provide helpful contacts in the field that may lead to full-time employment. If your college does not offer a work-study program and you can't find a paying summer job, consider volunteering at an appropriate government agency. The U.S. Geological Survey and the Bureau of Land Management usually have volunteer opportunities in select areas.

EMPLOYERS

According to the U.S. Department of Labor, almost two-thirds of the 56,000 surveying workers in the United States are employed in engineering, architectural, and surveying firms. Federal, state, and local government agencies are the next largest employers of surveying workers, and the majority of the remaining surveyors work for construction firms, oil and gas extraction companies, and public utilities. Only a small number of surveyors are self-employed.

STARTING OUT

Apprentices with a high school education can enter the field as equipment operators or surveying assistants. Those who have postsecondary education can enter the field more easily, beginning as surveying and mapping technicians.

College graduates can learn about job openings through their schools' placement services or through potential employers that may visit their campus. Many cities have employment agencies that specialize in seeking out workers for positions in surveying and related fields. Check your local newspaper or telephone book to see if such recruiting firms exist in your area.

ADVANCEMENT

With experience, workers advance through the leadership ranks within a surveying team. Workers begin as assistants and can move into positions such as senior technician, party chief, and, finally, licensed surveyor. Because surveying work is closely related to other fields, surveyors can move into electrical, mechanical, or chemical engineering or specialize in drafting.

EARNINGS

In 2005, surveyors employed in architectural and engineering services earned a mean annual salary of $48,480. According to the U.S. Department of Labor, the middle 50 percent of surveyors employed in all fields earned between $33,960 and $60,730 a year. The lowest 10 percent were paid less than $25,530, and the highest 10 percent earned over $75,870 a year. In general, the federal government paid the highest wages to its surveyors: $66,710 a year in 2005.

Most positions with the federal, state, and local governments and with private firms provide life and medical insurance, pension, vacation, and holiday benefits.

WORK ENVIRONMENT

Surveyors work 40-hour weeks, except when overtime is necessary to meet a project deadline. The peak work period is during the summer months, when weather conditions are most favorable. However, it is not uncommon for the surveyor to be exposed to adverse weather conditions.

Some survey projects may involve hazardous conditions, depending on the region and climate as well as plant and animal life. Survey crews may encounter snakes, poison ivy, and other plant and animal life and may suffer heat exhaustion, sunburn, and frostbite while in the field. Survey projects, particularly those near construction projects or busy highways, may impose dangers of injury from heavy traffic, flying objects, and other accidental hazards. Unless the surveyor is employed only for office assignments, the work location most likely will change from survey to survey. Some assignments may require the surveyor to be away from home for periods of time.

OUTLOOK

The U.S. Department of Labor predicts the employment of surveyors to grow about as fast as the average for all occupations through 2014. The outlook is best for surveyors who have bachelor's degrees and advanced field experience. Despite slower growth, the widespread use of technology, such as the Global Positioning System and Geographic Information Systems, will provide jobs to surveyors with strong technical and computer skills.

Growth in urban and suburban areas (with the need for new streets, homes, shopping centers, schools, gas, and water lines) will provide employment opportunities. State and federal highway improvement programs and local urban redevelopment programs also will provide jobs for surveyors. The expansion of industrial and business firms and the relocation of some firms to large undeveloped tracts will also create job openings. However, construction projects are closely tied to the state of the economy, so employment may fluctuate from year to year.

FOR MORE INFORMATION

For information on state affiliates and colleges and universities offering land surveying programs, contact
American Congress on Surveying and Mapping
6 Montgomery Village Avenue, Suite 403
Gaithersburg, MD 20879-3557
Tel: 240-632-9716
Email: info@acsm.net
http://www.acsm.net

For information on awards and recommended books to read, contact or check out the following Web sites:
American Association for Geodetic Surveying
6 Montgomery Village Avenue, Suite 403
Gaithersburg, MD 20879-3557
Email: aagsmo@acsm.net
http://www.aagsmo.org

National Society of Professional Surveyors
6 Montgomery Village Avenue, Suite 403
Gaithersburg, MD 20879-3557
Tel: 240-632-9716
http://www.nspsmo.org

For information on photogrammetry and careers in the field, contact
American Society for Photogrammetry and Remote Sensing
5410 Grosvenor Lane, Suite 210
Bethesda, MD 20814-2160
Tel: 301-493-0290
Email: asprs@asprs.org
http://www.asprs.org

For information on volunteer opportunities with the federal government, contact
Bureau of Land Management
Office of Public Affairs
1849 C Street, Room 406-LS
Washington, DC 20240-0001
Tel: 202-452-5125
http://www.blm.gov

U.S. Geological Survey
12201 Sunrise Valley Drive
Mail Stop 205P
Reston, VA 20192-0002
Tel: 888-275-8747
http://www.usgs.gov/volunteer

Urban and Regional Planners

QUICK FACTS

School Subjects
Business
English
Government

Personal Skills
Communication/ideas
Leadership/management

Work Environment
Primarily indoors
Primarily multiple locations

Minimum Education Level
Bachelor's degree

Salary Range
$34,920 to $63,700 to
$85,940+

Certification or Licensing
Voluntary

Outlook
About as fast as the average

DOT
199

GOE
11.03.02

NOC
2153

O*NET-SOC
19-3051.00

OVERVIEW

Urban and regional planners assist in the development and redevelopment of a city, metropolitan area, or region. They work to preserve historical buildings, protect the environment, and help manage a community's growth and change. Planners evaluate individual buildings and city blocks and are also involved in the design of new subdivisions, neighborhoods, and even entire towns. There are approximately 32,000 urban and regional planners working in the United States.

HISTORY

Cities have always been planned to some degree. Most cultures, from the ancient Greeks to the Chinese to the Native Americans, made some organized plans for the development of their cities. By the fourth century B.C., theories of urban planning existed in the writings of Plato, Aristotle, and Hippocrates. Their ideas concerning the issues of site selection and orientation were later modified and updated by Vitruvius in his *De architectura*, which appeared after 27 B.C. This work helped create a standardized guide to Roman engineers as they built fortified settlements and cities throughout the vast empire. Largely inspired by Vitruvius, 15th-century Italian theorists compiled enormous amounts of information and numerous ideas on urban planning. They replaced vertical walls with angular fortifications for better protection during times of war. They also widened streets and opened up squares by building new churches, halls, and palaces. Early designs were based on a symmetrical style that quickly became fashionable in many of the more prosperous European cities.

Modern urban planning owes much to the driving force of the Industrial Revolution. The desire for more sanitary living conditions led to the demolition of slums. Laws were enacted to govern new construction and monitor the condition of old buildings. In 1848, Baron George Eugene Haussmann organized the destruction and replacement of 40 percent of the residential quarters in Paris and created new neighborhood park systems. In England, the 1875 Public Health Act allowed municipalities to regulate new construction, the removal of waste, and newly constructed water and sewer systems.

THE JOB

Urban and regional planners assist in the development or maintenance of carefully designed communities. Working for government agencies or as consultants, planners are involved in integrating new buildings, houses, sites, and subdivisions into an overall city plan. Their plans must coordinate streets, traffic, public facilities, water and sewage, transportation, safety, and ecological factors such as wildlife habitats, wetlands, and floodplains. Planners are also involved in renovating and preserving historic buildings. They work with a variety of professionals, including architects, artists, computer programmers, engineers, economists, landscape architects, land developers, lawyers, writers, and environmental and other special-interest groups.

Chris Wayne works as a redevelopment planner for the city of Omaha, Nebraska. His work involves identifying new project sites—buildings that the planning department wants to redevelop—and going about acquiring the property. Before making a purchase, he hires an appraiser to determine the worth of the building and then makes an offer to the building's owner. If the owner accepts and the building is slated for redevelopment, the city may have to vacate the building. "This involves interviewing the residents," Wayne says, "to determine what's necessary for them to move. We determine what amount they'll be compensated." Various community programs assist in finding new housing or providing tenants with moving funds. Once the property has been vacated, the planning department accepts and reviews proposals from developers. A developer is then offered a contract. When demolition and construction begin, Wayne's department must monitor the project and make the necessary payments.

Urban and regional planners also work with unused or undeveloped land. They may help design the layout for a proposed building, keeping in mind traffic circulation, parking, and the use of open space. Planners are also responsible for suggesting ways to implement these programs or proposals, considering their costs and how to raise funds for them.

Schools, churches, recreational areas, and residential tracts are studied to determine how they will fit into designs for optimal usefulness and beauty. As with other factors, specifications for the nature and kinds of buildings must be considered. Zoning codes, which regulate the specific use of land and buildings, must be adhered to during construction. Planners need to be knowledgeable of these regulations and other legal matters and communicate them to builders and developers.

Some urban and regional planners teach in colleges and schools of planning, and many do consulting work. Planners today are concerned not only with city codes but also with environmental problems such as water pollution, solid waste disposal, water treatment plants, and public housing.

Planners work in older cities or design new ones. Columbia, Maryland, and Reston, Virginia, both built in the 1960s, are examples of planned communities. Before plans for such communities can be developed, planners must prepare detailed maps and charts showing the proposed use of land for housing, business, and community needs. These studies provide information on the types of industries in the area, the locations of housing developments and businesses, and the plans for providing basic needs such as water, sewage treatment, and transportation. After maps and charts have been analyzed, planners design the layout to present to land developers, city officials, housing experts, architects, and construction firms.

The following short descriptions list the wide variety of planners within the field.

Historic preservation planners use their knowledge of the law and economics to help preserve historic buildings, sites, and neighborhoods. They are frequently employed by state agencies, local governments, and the National Park Service.

Transportation planners, working mainly for government agencies, oversee the transportation infrastructure of a community, keeping in mind local priorities such as economic development and environmental concerns.

Housing and community development planners analyze housing needs to identify potential opportunities and problems that may affect a neighborhood and its surrounding communities. Such planners are usually employed by private real estate and financial firms, local governments, and community development organizations.

Learn More About It

Barnett, Jonathan. *Redesigning Cities: Principles, Practice, Implementation.* Chicago: American Planning Association, 2003.

Barrett, Carol. *Everyday Ethics for Practicing Planners.* Chicago: Planners Press, 2002.

Cavin, Andrew I. *Urban Planning.* New York: H. W. Wilson Company, 2003.

Jones, Warren W., and Natalie Macris. *A Career Worth Planning: Starting Out and Moving Ahead in the Planning Profession.* Chicago: Planners Press, 2000.

Levy, John M. *Contemporary Urban Planning.* 7th ed. Upper Saddle River, N.J.: Prentice Hall, 2005.

Riddell, Robert. *Sustainable Urban Planning: Tipping the Balance.* Boston: Blackwell Publishers, 2004.

Saunders, William S. *Urban Planning Today: A Harvard Design Magazine Reader.* Minneapolis: University of Minnesota Press, 2006.

Economic development planners, usually employed by local governments or chambers of commerce, focus on attracting and retaining industry in a specific community. They communicate with industry leaders who select sites for new plants, warehouses, and other major projects.

Environmental planners advocate the integration of environmental issues into building construction, land use, and other community objectives. They work at all levels of government and for some nonprofit organizations.

Urban design planners work to design and locate public facilities, such as churches, libraries, and parks, to best serve the larger community. Employers include large-scale developers, private consulting firms, and local governments.

International development planners specialize in strategies for transportation, rural development, modernization, and urbanization. They are frequently employed by international agencies, such as the United Nations, and by national governments in less developed countries.

REQUIREMENTS

High School

You should take courses in government and social studies to learn about the past and present organizational structure of cities and counties. You need good communication skills for working with people in a variety of professions, so take courses in speech and English composition. Drafting, architecture, and art classes will familiarize you with the basics of design. Become active on your student council so that you can be involved in implementing changes for the school community.

Postsecondary Training

A bachelor's degree is the minimum requirement for most trainee jobs with federal, state, or local government boards and agencies. However, more opportunities for employment and advancement are available to those with a master's degree. Typical courses include geography, public administration, political science, law, engineering, architecture, landscape architecture, real estate, finance, and management. Computer courses and training in statistical techniques are also essential. Most masters' programs last a minimum of two years and require students to participate in internships with city planning departments.

When considering schools, check with the American Planning Association (APA) for a list of accredited undergraduate and graduate planning programs. The APA can also direct you to scholarship and fellowship programs available to students enrolled in planning programs.

Certification or Licensing

Although not a requirement, obtaining certification in urban and regional planning can lead to more challenging, better-paying positions. The American Institute of Certified Planners, a division of the APA, grants certification to planners who meet certain academic and professional requirements and successfully complete an examination. The exam tests for knowledge of the history and future of planning, research methods, plan implementation, and other relevant topics.

Other Requirements

Chris Wayne pursued a master's in urban studies because he was drawn to community development. "I was interested in the social interaction of people and the space they occupy, such as parks and plazas," he says.

In addition to being interested in planning, you should have design skills and a good understanding of spatial relationships. Good analytical skills will help you in evaluating projects. Planners must be able to visualize the relationships among streets, buildings, parks, and other developed spaces and anticipate potential planning problems. As a result, logic and problem-solving abilities are also important.

EXPLORING

Research the origins of your city by visiting your county courthouse and local library. Check out early photographs and maps of your area to give you an idea of what went into the planning of your community. Visit local historic areas to learn about the development and history behind old buildings. You may also consider getting involved in efforts to preserve local buildings and areas that are threatened.

With the help of a teacher or academic adviser, arrange to interview a working planner to gain details of his or her job. Another good way to see what planners do is to attend a meeting of a local planning commission, which by law is open to the public. Interested students can find out details about upcoming meetings through their local paper or planning office.

EMPLOYERS

There are approximately 32,000 urban and regional planners working in the United States. Seven out of 10 of planners work for local governments; others work for state agencies, the federal government, and in the private sector.

Many planners are hired for full-time work where they intern. Others choose to seek opportunities in state and federal governments and nonprofit organizations. Planners work for government agencies that focus on particular areas of city research and development, such as transportation, the environment, and housing. Urban and regional planners are also sought by colleges, law firms, the United Nations, and even foreign governments of rapidly modernizing countries.

STARTING OUT

With a bachelor's degree, a beginning worker may start out as an assistant at an architectural firm or construction office. Others start out working as city planning aides in regional or urban offices. New planners research projects, conduct interviews, survey the field, and write reports on their findings. Those with a master's degree can enter the profession at a higher level, working for federal, state, and local agencies.

Work experience in a planning office or with an architectural or engineering firm is useful before applying for a job with city, county, or regional planning agencies. Membership in a professional organization is also helpful in locating job opportunities. These include the American Planning Association, the American Institute of Architects, the American Society of Civil Engineers, and the International City/County Management Association. Most of these organizations host student chapters that provide information on internship opportunities and professional publications. (See the end of this article for contact information.)

Because many planning staffs are small, directors are usually eager to fill positions quickly. As a result, job availability can be highly variable. Students are advised to apply for jobs before they complete their degree requirements. Most colleges have career services offices to assist students in finding job leads.

ADVANCEMENT

Beginning assistants can advance within the planning board or department to eventually become planners. The positions of senior planner and planning director are successive steps in some agencies. Frequently, experienced planners advance by moving to a larger city or county planning board, where they become responsible for larger and more complicated projects, make policy decisions, or become responsible for funding new developments. Other planners may become consultants to communities that cannot afford full-time planners. Some planners also serve as city managers, cabinet secretaries, and presidents of consulting firms.

EARNINGS

Earnings vary based on position, work experience, and the population of the city or town the planner serves. According to the U.S. Department of Labor, mean annual earnings of urban and regional planners employed in architectural and engineering services were $65,200 in 2005. The lowest 10 percent earned less than $34,920, and the highest 10 percent earned more than $85,940. Mean annual earnings in local government, the industry employing the largest numbers of urban and regional planners, were $55,690. According to an American Planning Association survey of its members, the median annual salary for planners was $63,700 in 2006. It also reported that its certified members earned an average of $13,000 more than those who were not certified.

Because many planners work for government agencies, they usually have sick leave and vacation privileges and are covered by retirement and health plans. Many planners also have access to city-owned automobiles.

Planners who work as consultants are generally paid on a fee basis. Their earnings are often high and vary greatly according to their reputations and work experience. Their earnings will depend on the number of consulting jobs they accept.

WORK ENVIRONMENT

Planners spend a considerable amount of time in an office setting. However, in order to gather data about the areas they develop, planners also spend much of their time outdoors, examining the surrounding land, structures, and traffic. Most planners work standard 40-hour weeks, but they may also attend evening or weekend council meetings or public forums to share upcoming development proposals.

Planners work alone and with land developers, public officials, civic leaders, and citizens' groups. Occasionally, they may face opposition from interest groups against certain development proposals, and, as a result, they must have the patience needed to work with disparate groups. The job can be stressful when trying to keep tight deadlines or when defending proposals in both the public and private sectors.

OUTLOOK

The U.S. Department of Labor expects the overall demand for urban and regional planners to grow about as fast as the average for all occupations through 2014. Communities turn to professional planners for help in meeting demands resulting from urbanization and the growth in population. Urban and regional planners are needed to zone and plan land use for undeveloped and rural areas as well as commercial development in rapidly growing suburban areas. There will be jobs available with nongovernmental agencies that deal with historic preservation and redevelopment. Opportunities also exist in maintaining existing bridges, highways, and sewers and in preserving and restoring historic sites and buildings.

Factors that may affect job growth include government regulation regarding the environment, housing, transportation, and land use. The continuing redevelopment of inner-city areas and the expansion of suburban areas will serve to provide many jobs for planners. However, when communities face budgetary constraints, planning departments may be reduced before others, such as police forces or education.

FOR MORE INFORMATION

For more information on careers, contact
American Institute of Architects
1735 New York Avenue, NW
Washington, DC 20006-5292
Tel: 800-242-3837
Email: infocentral@aia.org
http://www.aia.org

For more information on careers, certification, and accredited planning programs, contact
American Planning Association
122 South Michigan Avenue, Suite 1600
Chicago, IL 60603-6147
Tel: 312-431-9100
Email: CareerInfo@planning.org http://www.planning.org

For career guidance and information on student chapters as well as a list of colleges that offer civil engineering programs, contact
American Society of Civil Engineers
1801 Alexander Bell Drive
Reston, VA 20191-4400
Tel: 800-548-2723
http://www.asce.org

To learn about city management and the issues affecting today's cities, visit the association's Web site or contact
International City/County Management Association
777 North Capitol Street, NE, Suite 500
Washington, DC 20002-4290
Tel: 202-289-4262
http://www.icma.org

———————— INTERVIEW ————————

David Siegel is the president of the American Planning Association and director of planning and communications for Parametrix, Inc., in Portland, Oregon, where he manages community visioning, long-range planning, and growth management projects. He discussed his career and the field of planning with the editors of Careers in Focus: Architecture & Building.

Q. What are your main job responsibilities at Parametrix?

A. In my present job as director of planning and communications for Parametrix, my primary responsibilities are threefold:
- Project management
- Providing senior-level professional planning consultation on projects
- Business development

My secondary responsibilities include:
- Mentoring more junior-level staff
- Advising the development of business management practices

Q. How did you train to become a planning professional?

A. I have a bachelor's degree in political science and urban studies (Wittenberg University, Springfield, Ohio, 1974) and a master's degree in city and regional planning (Ohio State University, Columbus, Ohio, 1976). While an undergraduate student, I had an internship with the City of Cincinnati, Ohio (Department of Urban Development). As a graduate student, I had internships with the Ohio Department of Natural Resources and the Newfields Development Corporation.

Q. What are the most important personal and professional qualities for planning professionals?

A.
- Communications and public speaking. Bar none, this is the top skill to develop beyond your base level of planning expertise. If you can't communicate it, explain it, or facilitate discussion to address it, you might as well be a technician running models or making maps in the basement.
- Be a team player, willing to work with others, and responsible for delivering your project components/responsibilities on time.
- Be a proactive professional...a self-starter.
- Honesty
- Ethics
- Attention to detail

Q. What is the most important advice that you have to offer students as they graduate and look for jobs in this field?

A. • Develop a base resume, capable of being tailored for specific applications.

• Develop a statement of professional objectives for inclusion within the resume—again, tailoring it for the prospect at hand.

• Do your homework—learn the political and planning "lay of the land." What are the responsibilities of different agencies in an area? Who's doing what? Read the local newspaper or conduct some Web research.

• Conduct informational interviews with planners in agencies and consulting firms doing the type of work you'd like to be doing. It not only helps you make contacts; it helps give you an idea of the specific projects they're doing and gives them an idea of your capabilities and areas of interest. Follow the informational interview up with a handwritten thank-you note.

• Network. Get involved in professional organizations in your areas of interest. Build relationships. Volunteer for committees. Those you meet in this way will eventually be your peers, your clients, or your employer.

• Find a mentor (or two). Individuals who have been in the business a while can help you identify opportunities, avoid tar pits, and provide career advice in general. Learn from others!

Q. What is the future employment outlook for the field of planning?

A. The outlook is very, very good, depending on where you choose to locate. The market appears to be hot now and for the next couple of years—barring any recession. Employers are competing for quality employees. More and more communities are seeking to hire more consultants (to provide assistance in special areas of expertise or to help even out spikes of work) in order to keep long-term costs for training and health benefits in check.

Writers, Architecture & Construction

OVERVIEW

Writers express, edit, promote, and interpret ideas and facts in written form for books, magazines, trade journals, newspapers, technical studies and reports, company newsletters, radio and television broadcasts, and advertisements. Some writers specialize in a particular field, such as architecture and the construction industry. These professionals write stories about trends in construction, the architectural merits of a new public building, the increasing popularity of green building techniques, and countless other topics. There are approximately 142,000 salaried writers and authors employed in the United States.

HISTORY

The skill of writing has existed for thousands of years. Egyptian papyrus fragments from 3000 B.C. and Chinese books dating back to 1300 B.C. are some examples of early writing. During the Middle Ages, books—mostly religious in theme—were copied and illustrated by hand. The development of the printing press by Johannes Gutenberg in the middle of the 15th century and the liberalism of the Protestant Reformation, which helped encourage a wider range of publications, greater literacy, and the creation of a number of works of literary merit, helped develop the publishing industry. The first authors worked directly with printers.

QUICK FACTS

School Subjects
English
Journalism

Personal Skills
Communication/ideas
Helping/teaching

Work Environment
Indoors and outdoors
Primarily multiple locations

Minimum Education Level
Bachelor's degree

Salary Range
$24,320 to $46,420 to
$89,940+

Certification or Licensing
None available

Outlook
About as fast as the average

DOT
131

GOE
01.01.02

NOC
5121

O*NET-SOC
27-3043.00

The modern publishing age began in the 18th century. Printing became mechanized, and the novel, magazine, and newspaper developed. Several industries began to use magazines and journals as a way to disseminate information about their trade. Architecture and construction writers, in particular, turned their knowledge of the industry into stories and features for a variety of publications. Many large newspapers established sections devoted to the real estate market or the home and garden, and magazines targeted the public's

Architecture and Construction Publications on the Web

Architectural Digest
http://www.architecturaldigest.com

Architectural Record
http://archrecord.construction.com

Architecture
http://www.architecturemag.com

Building Design and Construction
http://www.bdcnetwork.com

Contract
http://www.contractdesign.com

Construction Equipment
http://www.constructionequipment.com

Engineering News-Record
http://www.enr.com

Environmental Design+Construction
http://www.edcmag.com

Interior Design
http://www.interiordesign.net

Landscape Architectural News Digest Online
http://www.asla.org/members/land

Landscape Architecture
http://www.asla.org/nonmembers/lam.cfm

Retail Construction
http://www.retailconstructionmag.com

interest in home design and styles such as *Home and Garden* and *Architectural Digest*. In addition, industry journals such as *Building Design and Construction* and *Landscape Architecture* were created to present new ideas, techniques, and advances to its members. Many architecture and construction writers may also contribute to online counterparts of print journals.

In addition to the print media, the broadcasting industry has contributed to the development of the professional architecture/construction writer. Radio, television, and the Internet are sources of information, education, and entertainment that provide employment for many writers, including those specializing in architecture and construction news.

THE JOB

Writers work in the field of communications. Specifically, they deal with the written word, whether it is destined for the printed page, broadcast, or computer screen. The nature of their work is as varied as the materials they produce: books, magazines, trade journals, newspapers, technical reports, company newsletters and other publications, advertisements, speeches, and scripts for radio and television broadcast. Writers develop ideas and write for all media.

Writers, reporters, or critics working for architecture- or construction-themed newspapers, magazines, and books share many of the same duties. First they come up with an idea for an article or book from their own interests or are assigned a topic by an editor. Reporters could be assigned to cover the campaign to save a once famous hotel from destruction or critique the ongoing renovation of a sports arena. Then writers begin gathering as much information as possible about the subject through library research, interviews, the Internet, observation, and other methods. They keep extensive notes from which they draw material for their project. Once the material has been organized and arranged in logical sequence, writers prepare a written outline. The process of developing a piece of writing is exciting, although it can also involve detailed and solitary work. After researching an idea, a writer might discover that a different perspective or related topic would be more effective, entertaining, or marketable.

When working on assignment, writers submit their outlines to an editor or other company representative for approval. Then they write a first draft of the manuscript, trying to put the material into words that will have the desired effect on their audience. They often rewrite or polish sections of the material as they proceed, always searching for just the right way of imparting information or expressing an idea or opinion. A manuscript may be reviewed, corrected, and revised numerous times before a final copy is submitted. Even after that, an editor may request additional changes.

Writers have a strong background in their specialty. For example, many architecture writers are renowned architects, which allows them to provide critical interpretations or analyses of different issues regarding the industry. Architecture and construction writers may write weekly columns in the Home or Real Estate section of a newspaper or submit stories for other sections as needed. Architecture and construction writers may also relay complicated industry information into material easily understood by the general public. Trade publications may have writers on staff or use articles written by freelancers. Some architecture and construction writers may be assigned to write scholarly material such as school textbooks or industry journals.

Those writing for the corporate world have a wide variety of responsibilities. Writers may work in such places as an architecture firm, construction firm, or real estate firm. They may be required to write news releases, annual reports, speeches for the company's president, or public relations materials. Typically, they are assigned a topic with length requirements for a given project. They may receive raw research materials such as statistics, and they are expected to conduct additional research, including personal interviews. Writers working in this environment must be able to write quickly and accurately on short deadlines, while also working with people whose primary job is not in the communications field. The written work is submitted to a supervisor and often a legal department for approval; rewrites are a normal part of the job.

REQUIREMENTS

High School

While in high school, build a broad educational foundation by taking courses in English, literature, foreign languages, history, general science, social studies, computer science, and typing. The ability to type is almost a requisite for all positions in the communications field, as is familiarity with computers.

Postsecondary Training

Competition for writing jobs almost always demands the background of a college education. Many employers prefer you have a broad liberal arts background or degree in English, literature, history, philosophy, or one of the social sciences. Other employers desire communications or journalism training in college. If you plan on specializing in architecture or construction, you should earn a degree, or at least minor, in architecture, construction, engineering, landscape design, interior design, or a related field. Occasionally, a master's degree in a specialized writing field may be required. A number of schools offer courses in journalism, and some of them offer courses or majors in book publishing, publication management, and newspaper and magazine writing.

In addition to formal course work, most employers look for practical writing experience. If you have served on high school or college newspapers, yearbooks, or literary magazines, you will make a better candidate, as well as if you have worked for small community newspapers or radio stations, even in an unpaid position. Many book publishers, magazines, newspapers, and radio and television stations have summer internship programs that provide valuable training if you want to learn about the publishing and broadcasting businesses. Interns do many simple tasks, such as running errands and answering phones, but some may be asked to perform research, conduct interviews, or even write some minor pieces.

Other Requirements

To be a writer, you should be creative and able to express ideas clearly, have a broad general knowledge, be skilled in research techniques, and be computer literate. You should also have a keen interest in architecture, construction, and related fields. Other assets include curiosity, persistence, initiative, resourcefulness, and an accurate memory. For some jobs—on a newspaper, for example, where the activity is hectic and deadlines are short—the ability to concentrate and produce under pressure is essential.

EXPLORING

As a high school or college student, you can test your interest and aptitude in the field of writing by serving as a reporter or writer on school newspapers, yearbooks, and literary magazines. Various writing courses and workshops will offer you the opportunity to sharpen your writing skills.

Small community newspapers and local magazines or trade publications often welcome contributions from outside sources, although they may not have the resources to pay for them. Jobs in bookstores, magazine shops, and even newsstands will offer you a chance to become familiar with various publications.

You can also obtain information on writing as a career by visiting local newspapers, industry trade magazines, publishers, or radio and television stations and interviewing some of the writers who work there. Career conferences and other guidance programs frequently include speakers on the entire field of communications from local or national organizations.

EMPLOYERS

There are approximately 142,000 writers and authors currently employed in the United States. Nearly 50 percent of salaried writers and editors work for newspaper, periodical, book, and directory publishers; radio and television broadcasting; software publishers; motion picture and sound-recording industries; Internet service providers, Web-search portals, and data-processing services; and Internet publishing and broadcasting, according to the *Occupational Outlook Handbook*. Writers are also employed by advertising agencies and public relations firms and for journals and newsletters published by business and nonprofit organizations, such as professional associations, labor unions, and religious organizations. Other employers are government agencies.

STARTING OUT

A fair amount of experience is required to gain a high-level position in the field. Most architecture and construction writers start out in entry-level positions. These jobs may be listed with college career services offices, or they may be obtained by applying directly to the employment departments of the individual publishers or broadcasting companies. Graduates who previously served internships with these companies often have the advantage of knowing someone who can give them a personal recommendation. Want ads in newspapers and trade journals are another source for jobs. Because of the competition for positions, however, few vacancies are listed with public or private employment agencies. The Construction Writers Association also lists job openings at its Web site, http://www.construction-writers.org/help.htm.

Employers in the communications field usually are interested in samples of published writing. These are often assembled in an organized portfolio or scrapbook. Bylined or signed articles are more credible (and, as a result, more useful) than stories whose source is not identified.

Beginning positions as a junior writer usually involve library research, preparation of rough drafts for part or all of a report, cataloging, and other related writing tasks. These are generally carried out under the supervision of a senior writer.

ADVANCEMENT

Most writers find their first jobs as editorial or production assistants. Advancement may be more rapid in small companies, where beginners learn by doing a little bit of everything and may be given writing tasks immediately. In large firms, duties are usually more compartmentalized. Assistants in entry-level positions are assigned such tasks as research, fact checking, and copyrighting, but it generally takes much longer to advance to full-scale writing duties.

Promotion into more responsible positions may come with the assignment of more important articles and stories to write, or it may be the result of moving to another company. Mobility among employees in this field is common. An assistant in one publishing house may switch to an executive position in another. Or a writer may switch to a related field as a type of advancement.

Freelance or self-employed writers earn advancement in the form of larger fees as they gain exposure and establish their reputations.

EARNINGS

In 2005, median annual earnings for salaried writers and authors were $46,420 a year, according to the U.S. Department of Labor. The lowest 10 percent earned less than $24,320, while the highest 10 percent earned $89,940 or more.

In addition to their salaries, many architecture and construction writers earn some income from freelance work. Part-time freelancers may earn from $5,000 to $15,000 a year. Freelance earnings vary widely. Full-time established freelance writers may earn up to $75,000 a year.

WORK ENVIRONMENT

Working conditions vary for architecture and construction writers. Although their workweek usually runs 35 to 40 hours, many writers work overtime. A publication issued frequently has more deadlines closer together, creating greater pressures to meet them. The work is especially hectic on newspapers, which operate seven days a week. Writers often work nights and weekends to meet deadlines or to cover a late-developing story.

Most writers work independently, but they often must cooperate with graphic designers, photographers, rewriters, and advertising people who may have widely differing ideas of how the materials should be prepared and presented.

Physical surroundings range from comfortable private offices to noisy, crowded newsrooms filled with other workers typing and talking on the telephone. Some writers must confine their research to the library or telephone interviews, but others may travel to other cities or countries or to local sites, such as construction sites, architecture museums, or other offices.

The work is arduous, but most architecture and construction writers are seldom bored. Some jobs require travel. The most difficult element is the continual pressure of deadlines. People who are the most content as writers enjoy and work well with deadline pressure.

OUTLOOK

The employment of all writers is expected to increase about as fast as the average rate of all occupations through 2014, according to the U.S. Department of Labor. The demand for writers by newspapers, periodicals, book publishers, and trade associations is expected to increase. The growth of online publishing on company Web sites and other online services will also demand many talented writers; those with computer skills will be at an advantage as a result. Advertising and public relations will also provide job opportunities. The U.S. Department of Labor predicts that the construction industry will continue to expand over the next decade. Talented writers will be needed to detail industry developments and trends for industry professionals, as well as the general public.

People entering this field should realize that the competition for jobs is extremely keen. Beginners, especially, may have difficulty finding employment. Of the thousands who graduate each year with degrees in English, journalism, communications, and the liberal arts, intending to establish a career as a writer, many turn to other occupations when they find that applicants far outnumber the job openings available. College students would do well to keep this in mind and prepare for an unrelated alternate career in the event they are unable to obtain a position as writer; another benefit of this approach is that, at the same time, they will become qualified as writers in a specialized field. The practicality of preparing for alternate careers is borne out by the fact that opportunities are best in firms that prepare business and trade publications and in technical writing.

FOR MORE INFORMATION

For information on writing careers in the construction industry, contact

Construction Writers Association
PO Box 5586
Buffalo Grove, IL 60089-5586
Tel: 847-398-7756
Email: office@constructionwriters.org
http://www.constructionwriters.org

This organization offers student memberships for those interested in opinion writing.

National Conference of Editorial Writers
3899 North Front Street
Harrisburg, PA 17110-1583
Tel: 717-703-3015
Email: ncew@pa-news.org
http://www.ncew.org

For information about working as a writer and union membership, contact

National Writers Union
113 University Place, 6th Floor
New York, NY 10003-4527
Tel: 212-254-0279
Email: nwu@nwu.org
http://www.nwu.org

For information on scholarships and student memberships aimed at those preparing for a career in technical communication, contact

Society for Technical Communication
901 North Stuart Street, Suite 904
Arlington, VA 22203-1821
Tel: 703-522-4114
Email: stc@stc.org
http://www.stc.org

This organization for journalists has campus and online chapters.
Society of Professional Journalists
Eugene S. Pulliam National Journalism Center
3909 North Meridian Street
Indianapolis, IN 46208
Tel: 317-927-8000
http://www.spj.org

Visit the following Web site for information on careers in construction:
Construct My Future
http://www.constructmyfuture.com

INTERVIEW

Jennifer Prokopy is a former president of the Construction Writers Association and the Principal of Orange Grove Media, LLC, an independent communications firm. (Visit http://www.orangegrove-media.com to read samples of her work.) She talked with the editors of Careers in Focus: Architecture & Building *about her career and the field of construction writing.*

Q. Tell us about your background and Orange Grove Media.

A. I founded Orange Grove Media, LLC in August 2002, with the goal of becoming a freelance writer. While my career focus had previously been on construction writing and marketing, my immediate goal in 2002 was not to become a full-time construction freelance writer—I wanted to write about the arts. But with all my contacts and experience in the construction field, it made logical sense, and I had clients right away, so I wound up focusing on construction, and I'm glad I did.

　　Before I had my own firm I was the media relations manager for Portland Cement Association (PCA), and I also was associate editor of Rock Products and Cement Americas magazines.

Q. What type of construction-related topics do you write about?

A. My favorite pieces are case studies, in which I examine a project from start to finish and offer readers a snapshot of what went well or wrong, and what the project partners learned. I like writing pieces that educate people and help them do better work in their field. My two primary areas of focus are concrete, and sustainable design and construction (or "green building").

Q. How did you train for this job? What was your college major or did you train in another way? Did you participate in any internships?

A. I received a BSJ from the Medill School of Journalism at Northwestern University. While there, I interned at a magazine, but not about construction. My first job out of college was at Rock Products and Cement Americas (then called Rock Products Cement Edition) magazines—they liked my interest in languages (Spanish and Chinese) because the emerging markets at that time were focused in Latin America and Asia. As part of my job there, I got to travel to China and write about its cement industry, which was amazing. Someone saw me present my findings at a trade show, and that's how I got my job at PCA.

Q. What are the most important personal and professional qualities for construction writers?

A. Professionally, attention to detail is important, and the desire to learn more than you think you should know. There is so much to learn about construction, and you have to be willing to dive in. You also have to have a flair for making the highly technical stuff make sense for the layperson—often, I am writing for an audience who doesn't know the difference between cement and concrete.

Personally, you need the same kind of people skills you use as a reporter in any field: You need to be friendly, engaging, and willing to talk to people from all walks of life. You encounter a lot of "characters" in construction, so you have to have a thick skin, because people will say offbeat things. But that's part of what makes the work so fun—you get to meet all kinds of interesting people. (If your secret wish is to become a novelist, these folks are the classic example of "material.")

Q. What are some of the pros and cons of your job?

A. I'm a freelance writer, so with that perspective in mind...

Pros: There's tons of stuff to write about, and construction is never going to stop—so there's always work. You can specialize and really enjoy a solid business in a niche. Because I've been in business for many years, I can pick and choose what I write about and who I work for. And I love working in my PJs.

Cons: Like any specialized writing, sometimes the topics can be overwhelmingly complicated. And sometimes it can get boring—so you have to mix up the different kinds of work.

And sometimes freelancing can get lonely; to combat that, I make sure and get out of the house every day at least once. And I started a small networking group for independent creatives—photographers, writers, graphic designers, Web developers—and we meet once a month. It's a great way to stay in touch with trends, make new friends, and build a network of people to work with.

Q. **What is the most interesting story that you have written and why?**

A. I wrote an advertorial supplement for Building Design & Construction on green building trends, and it was wonderful: lots of little stories making up a 16-page package. It was challenging and I learned a lot. I won an award from the Construction Writers Association for that project.

My second favorite: a story on inspecting historic structures for the ASHI Reporter. (ASHI is the American Society of Home Inspectors.) I learned so much and met a lot of interesting people, and because I live in a city with lots of old buildings, I took away knowledge that helps me appreciate local architecture and design on a deeper level.

Index

Page numbers in bold indicate major treatment of a topic.

A

administrative clerks 142
Air-Conditioning and Refrigeration Institute 98–99, 105
air-conditioning and refrigeration technicians 96
Air Conditioning Contractors of America 98, 105
American Academy of Environmental Engineers 90, 91, 93
American Association for Geodetic Surveying 158
American Association of University Professors 39
American Congress on Surveying and Mapping (ACSM) 155, 158
American Construction Inspectors Association 54
American Design Drafting Association (ADDA) 44, 48, 74, 75, 77
American Federation of Teachers 39
American Institute of Architects (AIA) 8, 11, 13, 166, 168
American Institute of Architecture Students 13
American Institute of Certified Planners 164
American Institute of Constructors (AIC) 56–57, 59, 62
American Planning Association (APA) 164, 166, 168
American Society for Photogrammetry and Remote Sensing 159
American Society of Civil Engineers 29, 166, 168
American Society of Heating, Refrigerating and Air-Conditioning Engineers Inc. 105–106
American Society of Home Inspectors 54
American Society of Interior Designers 129
American Society of Landscape Architects (ASLA) 133, 134, 136
American Society of Professional Estimators 65, 69
APVA Preservation Virginia 108
architects 5–13
  advancement 11
  earnings 11
  employers 9, 11
  employment outlook 12–13
  exploring the field 9
  high school requirements 7
  history 5
  industry stats 5
  information on 13
  job, described 6–7
  other career options 7
  overview 5
  postsecondary training 8
  requirements 7–9
  starting out 11
  work environment 11–12
Architectural Digest 172, 173
architectural drafters 72
Architectural Record 33, 172
Architectural Review 33
Architecture Careers 13, 39
Aristotle 160
Associated Builders and Contractors 98
Associated General Contractors of America 19, 22
Association for the Advancement of Cost Engineering International 65, 69
Association of Collegiate Schools of Architecture 13
Association of Construction Inspectors 54–55

B

Building and Construction Trades Department 62
Building Design and Construction 172, 173
building inspectors 49
buildings, tallest in the world 66
Bureau of Land Management 159
Burnham, Daniel 10

C

CAD designers 41
CAD engineers 41
CAD technicians. *See* computer-aided design drafters and technicians
Careers in Interior Design 130
Carll-White, Allison 129
Carmichael, Dennis 137–139
carpenters 14–22
  advancement 20
  earnings 20
  employers 19
  employment outlook 21
  exploring the field 19
  high school requirements 6
  history 14–15
  industry stats 14
  information on 22
  job, described 15–16
  overview 14
  postsecondary training 16–18
  requirements 16–18
  starting out 19
  work environment 20–21
cartographic drafters 72
checkers 72
Chemical & Engineering News 90

chief drafters 72
chief estimators 64
civil drafters 72
civil engineers 23–30
  advancement 27
  books about 26
  earnings 28
  employers 27
  employment outlook 29
  exploring the field 26–27
  high school requirements 25
  history 23–24
  industry stats 23
  information on 29–30
  job, described 24–25
  overview 23
  postsecondary training 25–26
  requirements 25–26
  starting out 27
  work environment 28–29
  See also environmental engineers
classes, architecture 34
cocooning 28
college professors, architecture 31–39
  advancement 37
  earnings 37–38
  employers 36
  employment outlook 38
  exploring the field 35–36
  high school requirements 34–35
  history 31–32
  industry stats 31
  information on 39
  job, described 32–34
  overview 1
  postsecondary training 35
  requirements 34–35
  starting out 36–37
  work environment 38
commercial designers 121
commercial drafters 72
computer-aided design drafters and technicians 40–48
  advancement 46
  earnings 46
  employers 45
  employment outlook 47–48
  exploring the field 44–45
  high school requirements 43
  history 40–41
  industry stats 40
  information on 48
  job, described 41–43
  overview 40
  postsecondary training 43–44
  requirements 43–44
  starting out 45
  work environment 46–47
computer-assisted drafters 72
construction electricians 79
construction engineers 25
construction foremen. *See* construction managers

construction industry, facts about 141
construction inspectors 49–55
  advancement 52–53
  earnings 53
  employers 52
  employment outlook 54
  exploring the field 52
  high school requirements 50
  history 49
  industry stats 49
  information on 54–55
  job, described 49–50
  overview 49
  postsecondary training 51
  requirements 50–52
  starting out 52
  work environment 53–54
Construction Management Association of America (CMAA) 59, 61, 62
construction managers 56–62
  advancement 61
  earnings 61
  employers 60
  employment outlook 62
  exploring the field 60
  high school requirements 58–59
  history 56–57
  industry stats 56
  information on 62
  job, described 57–58
  overview 56
  postsecondary training 59
  requirements 58–60
  starting out 60–61
  work environment 61
Construction Writers Association 176, 179
Construct My Future 145, 180
contract designers 121
contractors. *See* construction managers
Cool Careers 107
correspondence instructors 34
cost estimators 63–69
  advancement 67
  earnings 67–68
  employers 66
  employment outlook 68–69
  exploring the field 65–66
  high school requirements 64
  history 63
  industry stats 63
  information on 69
  job, described 63–64
  overview 63
  postsecondary training 65
  requirements 64–65
  starting out 67
  work environment 68
Council for Interior Design Accreditation (CIDA) 123, 124, 129
Council of Landscape Architectural Registration Boards (CLARB) 133, 137

D
da Rocha, Paulo Mendes 10
DeAngelis, Lee 86
De architectura (Vitruvius) 160
designers, architectural 6
detailers 72
de Wolfe, Elsie 121
Dezignare Interior Design Collective 130
distance learning instructors 34
drafters 70–77
advancement 75
earnings 76
employers 75
employment outlook 7
exploring the field 74–75
high school requirements 73
history 70–71
industry stats 70
information on 77
job, described 71–73
overview 70
postsecondary training 73–74
requirements 73–74
starting out 75
work environment 76–77

E
Ecole des Beaux-Arts 31–32
economic development planners 163
electrical drafters 72–73
electrical inspectors 50
electrical repairers 79
electricians 78–85
advancement 83
earnings 83–84
employers 82
employment outlook 84–85
exploring the field 82
high school requirements 80–81
history 78
industry stats 78
information on 85
job, described 79–80
overview 78
postsecondary training 81
requirements 80–82
starting out 82–83
work environment 84
elevator inspectors 50
Employment & Training Administration 151
energy conservation technicians 100
engineering-oriented technicians 100
Environmental Careers Organization (ECO) 86, 89, 90, 93
environmental engineers 86–93
advancement 91
books about 92
earnings 91
employers 90–91
employment outlook 92
exploring the field 90
high school requirements 89
history 86–87
industry stats 86
information on 92–93
job, described 87–89
postsecondary training 89
requirements 89–90
starting out 91
work environment 92
environmental planners 163
Environmental Protection Agency (EPA) 86, 87–88, 90, 91, 92, 99
estimators 6
extension work instructors 34

F
Federal Emergency Management Agency 155
field service representatives 103
file clerks 142
finish carpenters 14, 15
Frontiers 29
furnace installers 96

G
gas-appliance servicers 97
gas-burner mechanics 97
Gehry, Frank 10
geodetic computers 153
geodetic surveyors 153
Géométrie Descriptive (Monge) 71
geophysical prospecting surveyors 154
Gorrie, John 95
Griffin, Walter Burley 10
Gutenberg, Johannes 171

H
Habitat for Humanity 19, 22
Hadid, Zaha 10
Haussmann, George Eugene 161
heating and cooling technicians 94–107
advancement 102–103
earnings 103
employers 99–102
employment outlook 104–105
exploring the field 99
high school requirements 97
history 94–95
industry stats 94
information on 105–107
job, described 95–97
overview 94
postsecondary training 97–98
requirements 97–99
starting out 102
work environment 104
heating and refrigeration inspectors 50
heating and ventilating drafters 72
heating-equipment installers 96
highway surveyors 153
Hippocrates 160
Historic American Buildings Survey 113
historic places, endangered 110
historic preservationists 108–119
advancement 113
earnings 113

employers 112–113
employment outlook 114
exploring the field 112–113
high school requirements 111
history 108–109
industry stats 108
information on 114–115
job, described 109–111
overview 108
postsecondary training 111–112
requirements 111–112
starting out 113
work environment 114
historic preservation planners 162
Home and Garden 173
Home Builders Institute 22
housing and community development planners 162
Hunt, Richard Morris 32
HVAC Excellence 98, 99, 106

I

Independent Electrical Contractors Inc. 81, 83, 85
Institute of Electrical and Electronics Engineers, Inc. (IEEE-USA) 48
Institute of Transportation Engineers (ITE) 30
instrument assistants 153
Interior Design Educators Council 129–130
interior designers and decorators 120–130
advancement 126
earnings 127
employers 125–126
employment outlook 128–129
exploring the field 124–125
high school requirements 123
history 120–121
industry stats 120
information on 129–130
job, described 121–123
overview 120
postsecondary training 123–124
requirements 123–124
starting out 126
work environment 127–128
International Association of Machinists and Aerospace Workers 82
International Brotherhood of Electrical Workers 81, 82, 83, 85
International City/County Management Association 166, 168
International Code Council 51, 55
International development planners 163
International Federation of Professional and Technical Engineers 77
International Interior Design Association 128–129, 130
International Society of Certified Electronic Technicians 81, 85
International Union of Electronic, Electrical, Salaried, Machine, and Furniture Workers-Communications Workers of America 82

J

Jack J. Ryan and Sons Manufacturing Company 87, 88
Jefferson, Thomas 31
Jensen, Jens 10
job superintendents 6
Johnson, Philip 10
junior college architecture instructors 34
Junior Engineering Technical Society Inc. (JETS) 30, 93
JustCAD-Jobs.com 46

L

landscape architects 131–139
advancement 135
earnings 135
employers 134
employment outlook 136
exploring the field 133–134
high school requirements 132
history 131
industry stats 131
information on 136–137
job, described 132
overview 131
postsecondary training 132–133
requirements 132–133
starting out 134–135
work environment 136
Landscape Architectural Accreditation Board 133
Landscape Architectural News Digest Online 134, 172
Landscape Architecture 134, 172, 173
Landscape Architecture Interest Test 134
landscape drafters 72
land surveying managers 153
land surveyors 153
LAprofession.org 137
liaison representatives 100
Lincoln, Abraham 109

M

maintenance electricians 79
mapping engineers 24
marine surveyors 153
Massachusetts Institute of Technology (MIT) 31
McDonald, Bonnie 115–119
McKim, Charles Follen 32
mechanical drafters 72
mechanical inspectors 50
mine surveyors 153–154
Monge, Gaspard 71
Morgan, Julia 10

N

National Architectural Accrediting Board 8, 32
National Association of Environmental Professionals 93
National Association of Executive Secretaries and Administrative Assistants 145

National Association of Home Builders 19, 22, 98
National Association of Schools of Art and Design 123, 130
National Center for Construction Education and Research 62, 98
National Conference of Editorial Writers 179
National Council for Interior Design Qualification (NCIDQ) 124, 130
National Council for Preservation Education 111
National Council of Architectural Registration Boards (NCARB) 8, 9, 13
National Electrical Code 80, 81
National Electrical Contractors Association 85
National Historic Landmarks Program 113
National Historic Preservation Act 108, 109–110
National Joint Apprenticeship Training Committee 85
National Park Service (NPS) 109, 112, 113, 114, 162
National Preservation Institute 114–115
National Register of Historic Places 109, 113
National Society of Professional Surveyors 159
National Solid Wastes Management Association 93
National Trust for Historic Preservation 110, 112, 115, 116
National Writers Union 179
North American Technician Excellence Inc. 98, 106

O
office clerks 140–145
    advancement 143–144
    earnings 144
    employers 143
    employment outlook 144–145
    exploring the field 143
    high school requirements 142
    history 140–141
    industry stats 140
    information on 145
    job, described 141–142
    overview 140
    postsecondary training 142
    requirements 142–143
    starting out 143
    work environment 144
OfficeTeam 144, 145
oil-burner mechanics 97
oil-well directional surveyors 154
Olmsted, Frederick Law 10
orthographic projection 71

P
Partnership for Air Conditioning, Heating, and Refrigeration Accreditation 98, 106
Pei, I. M. 10
photogrammetric engineers 154

pipefitters 146–151
    advancement 149
    earnings 150
    employers 149
    employment outlook 150
    exploring the field 149
    high school requirements 148
    history 146
    industry stats 146
    information on 150–151
    job, described 146–148
    overview 146
    postsecondary training 148
    requirements 148–149
    starting out 149
    work environment 150
pipeline engineers 25
pipeline surveyors 154
Plato 160
plumbers 146–151
    advancement 149
    earnings 150
    employers 149
    employment outlook 150
    exploring the field 149
    high school requirements 148
    history 146
    industry stats 146
    information on 150–151
    job, described 146–148
    overview 146
    postsecondary training 148
    requirements 148–149
    starting out 149
    work environment 150
plumbing drafters 72
Plumbing-Heating-Cooling Contractors Association 98, 106, 150–151
plumbing inspectors 50
Pollution Engineering 90
Popcorn, Faith 128
Professional Surveyor Magazine 156
project managers 6
Prokopy, Jennifer 180–182
publications, architecture and construction 172
public works inspectors 50

R
Refrigerating Engineers & Technicians Association 98, 106
regional planners 160–170
    advancement 166
    books about 163
    earnings 166–167
    employment outlook 167–168
    exploring the field 165
    high school requirements 163–164
    history 160–161
    industry stats 160
    information on 168
    job, described 161–163

overview 160
postsecondary training 164
requirements 163–165
starting out 165–166
work environment 167
residential designers 121
rough carpenters 14, 15

S

sales managers 103
senior drafters 72
service managers 103
Sheet Metal and Air Conditioning Contractors'
National Association 107
Sheet Metal Workers International Association
98
Siegel, David 168–170
Society for Technical Communication 179
Society of Cost Estimating and Analysis
(SCEA) 65, 69
Society of Manufacturing Engineers 48
Society of Professional Journalists 180
specification writers 6
structural designers 6
structural drafters 72
structural engineers. *See* civil engineers
Student Conservation Association (SCA) 93
Sullivan, Louis 10
supervisors. *See* construction managers
surveying and mapping technicians 153
surveying engineers 24
surveyors 152–159
advancement 157
earnings 157
employers 156
employment outlook 158
exploring the field 156
high school requirements 154–155
history 152
industry stats 152
information on 158–159
job, described 153–154
overview 152
postsecondary training 155
requirements 154–156
starting out 156–157
work environment 157–158
Sutherland, Jackie 41–42, 43, 44

T

topographical drafters 72
tracers 72
transportation engineers 25
transportation planners 162

U

United Association of Journeymen and
Apprentices of the Plumbing and Pipefitting
Industry 98, 149, 151

United Brotherhood of Carpenters and
Joiners of America (UBCJA) 18, 19, 21,
22
urban design planners 163
urban planners 160–170
advancement 166
books about 163
earnings 166–167
employment outlook 167–168
exploring the field 165
high school requirements 163–164
history 160–161
industry stats 160
information on 168
job, described 161–163
overview 160
postsecondary training 164
requirements 163–165
starting out 165–166
work environment 167
U.S. Geological Survey 159
utility technicians 100
Utzon, Jorn 10

V

van der Rohe, Mies 10
Vitruvius 160

W

Washington, George 108
Waxman, Mike 86–87
Wayne, Chris 161, 164
Williams, Paul 10
window air-conditioning unit installers 96
window air-conditioning unit servicers 96
Worcester Polytechnic Institute 27, 29
Wright, Frank Lloyd 10, 32
**writers, architecture and construction
171–182**
advancement 177
earnings 177
employers 176
employment outlook 178–179
exploring the field 175–176
high school requirements 174
history 171–173
industry stats 171
information on 179–180
job, described 173–174
overview 171
postsecondary training 174–175
requirements 174–175
starting out 176–177
work environment 177–178